Called to
the One Hope

Samuel Kobia

Called to
the One Hope

A New Ecumenical
Epoch

WCC Publications, Geneva

Cover design: Marie Arnaud Snakkers

ISBN 2-8254-1489-1

© 2006, WCC Publications, World Council of Churches
P. O. Box 2100, 150 route de Ferney
1211 Geneva 2, Switzerland

Website: http://www.wcc-coe.org

No. 114 in the Risk Book Series

Printed in France

**To Philip Potter,
Ecumenist, mentor and friend, this book is dedicated**

When Philip was introduced as an honoured guest to the WCC assembly in Porto Alegre, Brazil in 2006, it was the ninth time he had attended, the only person there to have been at the 1948 assembly and all the others. The long-standing ovation he received was a tribute to this 85-year-old who was born on the West Indian island of Dominica.

Philip's first international ecumenical experience came in 1947 when he represented the Jamaica Student Christian Movement (SCM) at the World Conference of Christian Youth in Oslo. The next year he addressed the founding assembly of the WCC on behalf of the youth delegates. Philip's entire career in church service was spent in jobs related to mission or to the ecumenical movement. He joined the staff of the WCC youth department and in 1967 became director of the then Department of World Mission and Evangelism. In 1972, on the retirement of Eugene Carson Blake, he was appointed the WCC's third general secretary, a position he held until 1984 when he returned to the Caribbean. He is now living in his retirement at Lübeck, Germany, as the spouse of the bishop there, Bärbel Wartenberg-Potter.

Philip Potter was an eloquent and forceful speaker who seldom avoided the controversial nature of the biblical concern for the world and its suffering people. In a resolution honouring his retirement as general secretary, the central committee identified some of the main thrusts the Council owed to Potter's influence: "the insistence on the fundamental unity of Christian witness and Christian service which the gospel commends and makes possible, the correlation of faith and action, the inseparable connection between the personal spiritual life of Christian believers and their obedient action in the world."

Table of Contents

Preface

When the World Student Christian Movement of the previous century tried to understand what it meant to live the faith according to the Prophets and the Gospel, we were told to go out into the world with the Bible in one hand and the newspapers in the other. How were we to bring the Sermon on the Mount, for example, into the world and make it real for people if we did not know the agenda of the world? The ecumenical movement, I believe, does that best when it is not just being critical of the world, but also when it is being analytical through an engagement with reality.

I think there is no doubt that the 20th century was the ecumenical century. It was a time when there were good thinkers asking tough questions, pushing us to deepen our analysis so that we could become more forward-looking. We were weakest when we lost sight of that vision of the movement being in and for the world, especially after the [iron] curtain came down. Our vision was to hold up biblical justice and call the global structures of the world to be rooted in that justice. If there is no justice, there is no peace.

This simple but profound ethical and biblical imperative needs recovery as the ecumenical movement faces the third millennium which poses different problems, shifting loyalties, changing structures, reorientation and a new awareness of the calling of the churches. But, to do that we must ask what are we doing ourselves and in our churches to make this happen? There is no point in trying to transform the world if we are not willing to look at the movement and its member churches and see if they are willing to understand the world from a biblical and analytical perspective.

The same applies to the older mainline churches which have held privileged and sometimes immovable positions in the ecumenical movement. They also need transformation in a spirit of new development from the age of ecumenism in the 20th century whose basic stance was to hold high the banner of social justice. Now, in the 21st century, people must ask what did the "age of ecumenism leave behind for the leaders of the third millennium and what will the 21st century do with it?"

Personally, I am concerned that so little is being written of any depth, either theologically or philosophically, about God's will for the world. People are not asking hard questions. We are not hearing the voices of youth and of women challenging us to seek answers to their questions about where we are today and what we should do.

My colleague and friend, Sam Kobia, has written such a book as one of his immediate tasks following the last assembly. He has reviewed the assembly and raises the issues that must be faced following Porto Alegre. He also develops questions about what the ecumenical movement must face in today's world in language that is understandable and communicable. As he rightly says, we are moving into a new epoch of Christianity and the Council must move forward in terms of doing theology in a rapidly changing world and discern the areas of engagement that help to shape the future.

For all those Christians who are committed to the transformation of the world, in God's grace, this book, "Called to the One Hope" fills me with inspiration and hope for the future of the ecumenical movement and the witness of the churches.

Philip Potter,
Third General Secretary of the
World Council of Churches (1972-84)
June 17, 2006

Foreword

My friends will know that I am partial to the wisdom shared with me over the years by African elders. Often we would hear someone sum up a complex discussion or problem with a proverb. One of my favourites: "If you want to walk fast, walk alone. But if you want to go far, walk together with others".

When I became general secretary of the World Council of Churches in 2003, the planning and theme for the ninth assembly were already under way. It struck me that this huge meeting to be held in less than three years – the first ever in Latin America, the first ever with an African general secretary, the first of the third millennium – was similar in some ways to the first assembly in 1948, but also vastly different in style and circumstance. Christianity, the world, the churches and the ecumenical movement had changed in less than 60 years beyond anything our founders could have imagined in their wildest dreams.

Konrad Raiser, my predecessor, I knew well had spent 10 years trying to push a reluctant institution to face the many changes demanding the attention of the churches in the world. It is a scary world out there: huge insecurity amidst obscene affluence in some parts of the world; massive poverty, disease and violence for billions of others. Globalization and a single superpower have revived the imperial agenda in post-modern garb. People are insecure, frightened, uncertain and the traditional institutional churches cannot seem to meet these needs. I felt this in my own continent where poverty and disease and war have left people filled with anxiety and fear. But, I also sensed the insecurity amidst plenty in Europe where I now live in one of the most affluent countries in the world.

Where, I kept asking myself, is the hope? Why are so many people feeling such malaise about their future? It is not just the current misnamed war on terrorism or globalized poverty and disease, or the planet's tragic environmental devastation. It is a loss of faith, of belief. What can the ecumenical movement do to bring hope to a hopeless world, not the false hope of denial or the vapid spirituality that escapes reality but the flame of hope that is willing to accept the challenges of the 21st century?

I recalled the ecumenical movement's history and its passion for unity. Its offer of the hope that so many were yearning for after the horrors of World War II. The dynamism and energy that sent us into active humanitarian relief during the mass starvation of Biafra and the optimism and passion that we showed during the long days of apartheid in South Africa.

Shortly before I became general secretary, I wrote a book about Africa and the calling of a new vision for the church there. It is entitled "The Courage to Hope". Now, I was preparing for a new job, a critical assembly and there was that word, again – Hope. How could we, in the ecumenical movement, find the courage to hope in the midst of such a bleak world?

Why not find out, I thought, as I pondered the future. So, in those early months as general secretary, I made a critical decision to visit all the regions in the world wherever Christians were wrestling with change. This would be my priority above all other priorities. It was an exhausting journey and an exhaustive plan, which was only completed in 2005. I spoke quite often to concerned people but I also listened intently everywhere I went. I began with Africa in 2004 where churches joined with the people of Rwanda in confessing our failure to act fearlessly 10 years previously during the genocide of almost a million people.

As an African ecumenist for much of my life, I tried to be culturally sensitive wherever I went and find the courage to tell the churches that a status quo ecumenical movement and Council were no longer an option. Each time I came back to my Geneva office, it was almost as a visitor from afar. People around the globe helped reinforce my sense that alienation and a loss of identity made fertile ground for the fear and malaise that were gripping societies and which the ecumenical movement seemed unable to challenge. As traditional Protestantism in the West was being weakened by secularism, the centre of ecumenism had shifted to the South.

Formation became a crucial point in visit after visit. Traditional youth and lay training centres supported by Protestants in Europe had been the training ground for the early ecumenical movement. Now the evangelical and Pentecostal youth movements are alive with energy and dynamism but they were not with us. Where, I wondered, are our future ecumenical leaders to be formed? Even though I found everywhere a hunger for spirituality, the gnawing and difficult question arose: have we in the WCC become too institutionalized and too bureaucratized, to respond in 21st century terms to this yearning for healing and wholeness?

Movements are thriving while institutions are languishing. These have a vitality and openness lacking in our structures. We are over-cautious, we are afraid of offending.

I also visited the Ecumenical Patriarch of Constantinople, Bartholomew I, and the new Pope, Benedict XVI, who are essential to the quest for visible unity. The heads of these ancient and holy churches reiterated each their commitment to the one ecumenical movement and I encouraged them to do even more by increasing their support, including financially, for the endeavours of the World Council of Churches. The new volatile and dynamic churches of the Global South are challenged to become more involved in the ecumenical movement. The evangelicals and Pentecostals remain outside in most cases. More questions.

To what extent is the Global Christian Forum really meeting the objective of the broadening of the fellowship? A serious evaluation must be carried out following the Forum's second global meeting in 2007. Are we willing to make the costly and painful compromises entailed in creating something new? Behold I make all things new, said Jesus, but he was willing to make the sacrifices. Are we willing to give up, for example, our rigid concept of membership? Our insistence that all assistance must be made on the basis of need alone? These structures of security we have erected – are they of God, or are they of the corporate world where professionalism, competition, internal politics, promotions and status are the motivation?

So many questions. So little time. Can it all be sustained? Global confessional and denominational bodies and ecumenical institutions have always been able to find support but the time is nigh when these institutionalized structures cannot be sustained. Churches may well be forced to make choices: denominationalism or ecumenism? Who knows, but we need to decide. All these questions – and many others – are central to discerning the future of ecumenism in the 21st century.

This book "Called to the One Hope" comes at a critical time of change in the ecumenical movement and the world. It follows quickly after our Porto Alegre assembly. Its genesis began during my two years of travels and from listening to people from many different backgrounds, cultures and churches. Stories of their yearnings and their questions about how the ecumenical vision can be made real in this third millennium, in this new epoch of humanity are reflected. The church can be the church again, the ecumenical movement can rekindle the flame of hope, it can if it is willing to accept the challenge of change.

As the book describes, the future anxieties are at least as great as those faced by the first assembly of the WCC. That is why I say in St Paul's words that we are called to the one hope (Eph. 4:4). It is a different world, a different movement and the work for transformation is daunting. We can face the future directly and honestly or we can turn further inwards and fail in our mission to offer hope.

Samuel Kobia,
General Secretary, WCC,
Geneva, 2006

Introduction

Celebrating Life – *a festa da vida*

God, in your grace, transform the world. This theme (the theme of the WCC's ninth assembly held in Porto Alegre, Brazil, in February 2006) has come alive to me during my visits to member churches in the past two years.

And, here in Latin America, we celebrated with the people the election of Michelle Bachelet as the first woman President of Chile and Evo Morales as the first Indigenous President of Bolivia. Commenting on these historic developments, one Latin American ecumenical friend told me, "this signifies that the seeds of peace, justice and democracy which were planted 20 or 30 years ago have grown up through the years and are now blooming". That reminded me of the moving experiences I had during my visit to South America in November of 2004.

One particular moment was in Buenos Aires, Argentina. The leadership of the Mothers and Grandmothers of the Plaza de Mayo told me that under the dictatorships of the mid-1970s, churches and ecumenical organizations provided the 'safe place' where the relatives of those who disappeared could meet to share their sorrow and hope. One could not hold back her tears as she said that if it had not been for such accompaniment, most likely she would not be here to tell her story. But what were really impressive for me were the testimonies. For over 30 years they have lifted the flame of hope, seeking truth and justice. The crucible of their spirit is matched only by their incredible resilience.

In my travels to all regions of the world, I witnessed again and again such surprising signs of hope. People celebrate life in places where humanly speaking one could only see death and despair. It is this capacity to celebrate together and to strengthen life in community that has kept Africa going. It reminds me of what links my own experiences as an African with the history of Brazil and of this continent from the days of the slave trade. In the lively and vital celebration of the carnival, I catch glimpses of my African heritage.

As a Christian, I discern the gift of God's grace in those moments, when life is transformed and hope becomes reality.

It is against such a backdrop that I dream of an ecumenical movement as a movement of people who are messengers of God's grace, a people open to each other and discovering the presence of Christ and of God's grace in the other. To see Christ in the other is so much stronger than all that separates us. The reward in the search for visible unity of the churches in Christ is to discover the presence of the grace of God in each other on the common journey as we walk together. I make five assertions of an ecumenical movement open to these signs of God's transformative grace as a movement of life:

- grounded in spirituality;
- takes ecumenical formation and youth seriously;
- dares to work for transformative justice;
- puts relationships at the centre; and
- takes risks to develop new and creative ways of working.

We came to Porto Alegre to reflect, to deliberate, to discuss, and to make decisions. But most of all, we came together to pray for unity of the churches and the world, to rejoice in the shared experience of glorifying God in Christ, and to affirm the deep spiritual bond that holds us together across many differences. Imagine a time 10 years hence when this assembly has long been over: what will we remember above all else? Most probably, the common prayers in the worship tent, the murmur of the Lord's prayer being said in 100 different languages; and the exhilarating feeling of this assembly, in all of its glorious diversity gathered to praise God who has given us life. Think of the spiritual base of the ecumenical movement as the *festa da vida* – the feast of life.

The invitation to the feast comes from God and we are all welcome. This feast, this festa, comes to us as grace. The wonder of grace is that it is a gift, which we don't deserve, a reward which we don't earn, but it is freely given and is ours for the partaking. In the Christian tradition, grace is defined as a spiritual, supernatural gift which human beings receive from God without any merit on their part. Grace can better be defined as signs and, indeed, acts of divine love. *Festa da vida. Fiesta de la vida.* The feast of life. *Fête de la vie. Fest des Lebens. Karamu la maisha.*

As churches, we celebrate the life-giving presence of God among us in the Holy Eucharist. It is at the Lord's table that the broken body of Christ and the blood shed on the cross create a new community reconciled with God. This Eucharistic vision of the world, reconciled and united with God in Christ, is at the heart of the visible unity of the church which we seek. Spiritual discernment is essential for our way towards unity.

When I talk of spirituality, I want to make it clear that I am not referring merely to contemporary religious or quasi-religious responses to the felt lack of a deeper meaning in the values of affluent societies. I point to the subject and origin of all life: God's Holy Spirit. All our efforts will be meaningless and powerless if they are not blessed by God's loving grace. After such blessings, one's spiritual life is fully transformed. One's intellect, will and memory are ever more focused on God.

In this fractured and insecure world the forces of globalization and militarism threaten life itself. Being in touch with the word of God and experiencing the presence of God in the other makes us able to withstand the day-to-day rigours of working for peace and justice. The 'business' of our meetings is part of the process of spiritual discernment and is embedded in the *festa da vida*. The assembly could be looked at as a spiritual experience and not just as a business meeting to fulfil a constitutional mandate.

Hence the ninth assembly was the first to use consensus procedures. Consensus is an effort to build the common mind. The differences among us reflect the realities of our congregations and the lives that we share with people around us. These differences help us see the multi-faceted realities and lead us to search for the truth that is not ours, but the truth of the Holy Spirit among us (1 John 5:6). We approached consensus not as a technique but as a process of spiritual discernment.

We live in a world of proliferating churches and organizations, resurgent confessionalism, a shift of the centre of

Christianity to the South, painful internal struggles within church families, the growth of Pentecostal, evangelical, conservative and charismatic churches. In mainline Western churches, once the mainstay of ecumenical councils, here are complex patterns of shifting membership. A clear vision of what these churches may become is still emerging. All of these trends and uncertainties have made the ecumenical movement fragile.

Young people grow up in this reality, struggling for orientation and meaning. The ecumenical movement emerged from the same search for new meaning by an earlier generation of young people. The heritage of those who came before us is too precious to be kept just for us. It must be transmitted to the next generation. We pledged to devote energy and commitment to nurturing a new generation, knowing that this is not just a matter of education and formation, but of trust and participation.

Ecumenical formation is based on the formation of faith. Ecumenical learning is experiential. Young people need opportunities to experience the joy of working and praying with others from different traditions and different contexts. They need support and mentoring to participate fully in ecumenical gatherings with their intimidating elders. We need to change to respond to the demands of young people. At a time when information technology is forever advancing, we must enable our youth to interact more deeply and to discover creative ways of using virtual spaces for ecumenical formation. The time has come when we must not only open opportunities to young people for their ecumenical growth and leadership, but where we must learn from the innovative and dynamic models of ecumenical relationships that youth can teach us. As an ecumenical and intergenerational family, we need to humble ourselves and to listen to young people. It was with young people that the ecumenical movement was born. It is young people's passion and insight today that will ensure its relevance and vitality. Without young people our ecumenical family is incomplete. Young people need to know that they are important partners. They can help all of us to understand better where we are going and what kind of response is required of us. It is young people today who increasingly have little patience with the divisions among us and who reach out to others with similar values. There is a widespread hunger for spirituality in young people, even though there may be a rejection of church structures. Out of desperation, one of my colleagues enlisted her 22-year-old daughter to format the assembly *mutirâo* workshop schedule over last Christmas. When she finished the tedious work with Excel spreadsheets, she said excitedly to her mother, "I want to come to this assembly. The workshops are so diverse and so interesting – I had no idea that this was what ecumenism is all about. It makes me want to get involved."

The *festa da vida* is a call to young people. The *festa da vida* is an open feast, but sometimes participating in an open feast means that others must step back. I challenged all church leaders at the assembly to look at ways that young people can participate. We tried hard to make Porto Alegre a youth assembly, but only partly succeeded.

It is in Jesus Christ that God's grace transforms the world from within. Christ became flesh, lived among us and shared human suffering and joy (John 1:14). In him and through him all were created and all are called together in unity, in justice and peace. In him, all are to be reconciled, transformed, transfigured and saved (Col 1:15-23): a new humanity and a new heaven and earth (Rev 21:1). The whole world is filled with God's grace in the life-giving power of the Holy Spirit. Such emphasis on God's transformative grace corresponds to a new emphasis on transformative justice.

God has given us the gift of life and we have abused it. Human greed and thirst for power have created structures that cause people to live in terrible poverty. Our world's climate is in jeopardy. In an era when there is more than enough food to go around many times over, 852 million people are hungry. Every single day, 25,000 people die of hunger. Every day, more than 16,000 children die from hunger-related causes – one every five seconds. Globalization both brings us closer together than ever before – and exacerbates disparities of power and wealth. Violence continues to cause untold suffering – violence in the homes, on our streets, in our countries, even in our churches.

Something is gravely wrong when at the beginning of the 21st century the wealth of the three richest individuals on earth surpassed the combined annual GDP of the 48 least developed countries. Political arguments and economic rationalizations cannot counter the basic immorality of a world with this degree of inequality.

Something is gravely wrong in the world when there is still a real risk that nuclear weapons will be used in our lifetimes. Nuclear proliferation is an outrage to all humanity. The recent reports of countries acquiring nuclear weapons technology are frightening. But it is equally a scandal that countries which possess vast arsenals of nuclear weapons are unwilling to renounce their use.

Something is horribly wrong when children are sold into prostitution, when babies are aborted because they are girls, and when people of a certain ethnicity or race or caste or religion continue to be oppressed. We need to be spiritually-centred to confront such realities.

As churches, we are called to plan together, to speak together and to take action together in the face of conditions that we know to be wrong. A belief in God's call for abundant life means affirming human dignity and the right of the poor to liberate themselves from unjust conditions. The struggle for life must be rooted in the experiences and the actions of those who are oppressed and excluded. When the poor as social actors begin to disappear behind 'poverty' as defined by the statistics of the international financial institutions, our whole understanding changes. Poverty becomes an abstract term, divorced from the reality of what it means to be people who are poor. We must struggle to hold up the voices of the poor, to recognize them as actors in their own struggles, and to strive continually to enable them to advocate on their own behalf.

The feast of life is not a party. It is a celebration of life, which will sometimes be painful. The *festa da vida* invites all into the household of God, to experience the pain and the suffering of others. The vision of Christians gathered around a table in celebration recalls the gospel accounts of the last supper. This is the source of our Eucharistic vision, an occasion for joy.

And yet at the very same time, the disciples sensed that something was amiss. There was a failure of mutual trust, a prophecy of betrayal, a conviction that something was terribly wrong. When Jesus confirmed that one of them would betray him, the response on the lips of each was, "Is it I, Lord?" And this question was not directly answered – for even though 11 of the 12 would not betray him, all would deny him. In today's world, we find that our celebration of being together is also marked by contradictions, by a lack of mutual trust, by failure to live up to the Gospel call. Is it I, Lord? Is it we? As part of humanity we must constantly ask why the world is in such a mess. We need to move from resignation to indignation to righteous anger.

If we are to transform the world, we have to change our paradigms. For example, it is common practice these days to talk about the United States as the world's sole superpower. And yet we know that the powers of this world and the empires they form come and go in history. At the end, the Bible tells us, they are built on feet of clay. As we are recognizing, power is not only expressed in different forms of empire. The rapid development of newly emerging technologies is a powerful tool with great potential impact on people and nature.

When there are such enormous inequalities and unequal access to different means of power, it counts in what part of the world one lives. Our churches and the stance they take on matters of economic justice and other ethical challenges often reflects the realities surrounding them and impacting on the lives of their members. Some churches tend to see the present phase of economic globalization as the continuation of 500 years of oppression through colonialism and changing empires. Others emphasize change and discontinuity based on their experience of the rapidly changing political landscape. These different perspectives cannot be easily reconciled.

At the assembly we celebrated the mid-term of the Decade to Overcome Violence. The goal of DOV is not so much to eradicate violence as it is to overcome the spirit, the logic and the practice of violence by actively seeking reconciliation and peace. This is an ecumenical task because, as we are learning, preventing violence cannot be accomplished by any particular group. Preventing and overcoming violence must be done collaboratively by churches together, and jointly in cooperation with governmental and civic institutions and people's grassroots initiatives.

In the second half of the Decade, several issues must be considered. Firstly, globalization is a reality on every level, not just economic. Terrorism appears to be globally networked, as is the war on terrorism. The consequences of this affect people in their activities and dignity almost everywhere. We must, therefore, take globalization and its many implications into consideration as we plan our common actions towards proclaiming the good news of peace. Secondly, interfaith dialogue and cooperation are significant and imperative in the process towards overcoming violence, seeking peace and promoting reconciliation. Churches and religious people of all walks of faith recognize the imperative of interfaith action in response to the pressing needs and concerns of the societies in which they live. More and more people see interfaith action as an integral part of the ecumenical task. The vision of today is that God's *oikoumene* includes not just Christians, but people of all faiths.

Thirdly, spirituality contributes crucially to overcoming violence and building peace. I believe that prayer and contemplation together form the foremost discipline for overcoming violence. The joint exercise of that spiritual discipline is an ongoing challenge for our fellowship.

Within this dimension of spirituality, I am grateful to our Orthodox brothers and sisters in helping the ecumenical movement to recognize the dimension of the earth and nature more consistently. Our spirituality is robbed of a crucial dimension if it does not include our being part of creation as well as co-creators in an intimate relationship with God's earth and all that fills it.

The theme of the ninth assembly – "God, in your grace, transform the world" – reminds me very much of the theme of the first assembly in 1948 in Amsterdam: "Man's disorder and God's design". The theme of the Amsterdam assembly reflected both the violent past and the new hopes of the time. The colonial conquest of European nations had reached into the most distant corner of the world. European nations turned against each other in violence in two world wars. With the development and use of the atomic bomb, humanity had acquired the terrible capacity to destroy life on this planet. The vital question of the new era was whether God's design of a transformed world would mark the future or whether human disorder where life is threatened and millions suffer would prevail.

The theme of the Amsterdam assembly reflected a certain optimism that responsible leadership mindful of God's design would correct the disorder of human societies. Such optimism – often unaware of its contextual origins in Europe and North America and its colonial and imperial connotations – was fuelled by the rapid development of new technologies at the cutting edge of economic, political and military power.

Just as in Amsterdam, we too are on the threshold of a new era, conscious of the enormous gap between God's will for humanity and the present reality. In the run-up to the Amsterdam assembly, the world stood on the brink of a human-generated disaster; in the run-up to the Porto Alegre assembly, the world also stood on the brink of seemingly endless human-made natural disasters. According to God's design nature has an in-built self-regulatory capacity. But, driven by insatiable greed, human beings have interfered with God's design to such an extent as to induce disasters capable of annihilating all life. Today we have become much more aware that the crisis goes far deeper and manifests itself beyond injustice and war among human beings, affecting all life.

In particular, I point to the challenge to this planet and all its species of climate change. Just as atomic weapons changed the very way we thought about life, so too the potential of major climatic changes puts all life as we know it in danger.

Climate change is, arguably, the most severe threat confronting humanity today. This is not an issue for the future: severe consequences are already being experienced by millions of people. We must call on all Christian churches to speak to the world with one voice in addressing the threat of climate change.

This divided world needs a church living as one body of Christ. Archbishop Desmond Tutu once said "apartheid is too strong for a divided church". I say that this planet, where all life is threatened, needs a church which lives unity in diversity as a sign and foretaste of the community of life that God wants to be – God's household of life, the inhabited earth, the *oikoumene*. We are created one humanity and one earth community by the grace of God.

Together with the Decade to Overcome Violence, the Africa Focus was a major mandate from the eighth assembly. In response to the call from the African plenary at Harare, the WCC committed itself to accompany the churches and the people of Africa on their "journey of hope" for a better Africa. In the intervening years the Ecumenical Focus on Africa provided the framework for coordinated programmatic work in the areas of women and youth, peacebuilding, governance and human rights, reconstruction, HIV and AIDS, people with disabilities, theological education and ecumenical formation, inter-religious relations, church and ecumenical relations and economic justice. (The full account is found in the official report *From Harare to Porto Alegre* and in the WCC book *Journey of Hope*, launched during the Porto Alegre assembly.)

The insights gained from our experience with the Ecumenical Focus on Africa suggest that overcoming poverty in Africa, which should be a high priority in our future ecumenical accompaniment, will require addressing two root causes: one systemic and structural, the other ethical and political. On the systemic level, there are four factors that combine to militate against food sufficiency, which is a prerequisite to overcoming poverty: (1) the economic policies which are unfavourable to investment in agriculture and rural community development; (2) rural-urban migration which continues to empty rural areas of educated and able-bodied young people who contribute the core of human resources for rural transformation; (3) violence, which includes civil war and senseless inter-personal violence at the domestic and community level; and (4) the most recent is HIV and AIDS in sub-Saharan Africa. For aid to make a dent on poverty in Africa it must be an integral part of a holistic and comprehensive approach addressing all those factors. The experience so far has shown that overcoming poverty and achieving social transformation is more than a mechanical approach to sustainable development. A vital ingredient that lacks is the moral will on the part of African leadership. For far too long African leaders have accepted the unacceptable and tolerated the intolerable.

Progressively, Afro-pessimism is being replaced by guarded optimism on the part of African churches and African people. The transformation from the Organization for African Unity to the African Union (AU), the creation of new partnerships in Africa's development, the ongoing transformation of the All Africa Conference of Churches (AACC) into a strategic ecumenical instrument, peace initiatives of women in Sierra Leone and Sudan and the recent election of the first woman president in Africa, Ellen Johnson-Sirleaf as President of Liberia, are signs of hope. But, in the final analysis, Africa remains a paradox: it is extremely rich, yet full of extremely poor people. In the last 30 years a staggering $US 330 billion has been poured into Africa. So why is Africa in its present predicament? Financial aid alone is not the answer to overcoming poverty in Africa; it is too easily misconceived, misdirected, misregulated or misapplied. It will take a level and depth of anger, similar to that which produced the spirit of Pan-Africanism in the struggle against colonialism and apartheid, to overcome poverty in Africa. The Africans on the continent and the African diaspora will have to come together again under the rubric of a kind of global Africana and say: it cannot go on like this because what is at stake is the core of what it means to be African – the African soul!

Why is it so difficult to overcome what separates us? Why do we still fall short in our relationships with other human beings despite the technological advances of our age that defy imagination? It is incredible to think of our ability to manipulate genes and to send rockets to the far reaches of our solar system – while we are still engaged in wars.

There is a common element in the social, economic and environmental threats to life we are confronted with and the ambiguous experience of growing inter-dependence that provokes greater fragmentation and enmity instead of better cooperation. Fears and anxieties prevent us from a common witness. The biggest challenges that we face today all converge in the lack of human capacity to relate to each other, to creation, and to God. Whether we talk about social realities, issues of power and politics, and even about the realities within and among the churches, we can see that the quality of our relationships has suffered considerably for decades and centuries.

We live in a diverse world – a world of ethnic, racial, linguistic, cultural and religious differences. Our societies have become multi-cultural. And yet our capacity to relate to the other is sadly limited. We lash out and accuse those who are different from us. We are too often fearful of newcomers. We draw lines between others and ourselves in ways that are hurtful. Racism continues to rear its ugly head; xenophobia and Islamo-phobia spread to more and more places; anti-Semitism has revived where it was expected to have died years ago. And yet the commonalities that unite us are far greater than those that divide us. We are all capable of love, we all revere our families, we all depend on the environment, and we all have a vested interest in making this planet a loving and hospitable place.

If we focus on our capacity to relate to each other, to creation and to God, we realize that our ethical challenges have a profoundly spiritual dimension. We can no longer separate ethics and ecclesiology, the search for unity of the church and the unity of humankind. They are closely intertwined with each other. The reality of sin reflects the reality of broken relationships with God, the fellow human being and creation. Sin – so teaches the Bible – is first and foremost a matter of broken relationships in all of these three dimensions of our existence. Sin is real. Sin has its social and practical expressions, which breed death instead of life and undermine our fellowship. Christ restores life and heals and reconciles relationships distorted by sin. We celebrate this mystery of life renewed in Christ in the Eucharist that transforms us as members of the one body of Christ. In our daily lives, the Eucharist continues in the healing of relationships, in sharing life with life. For Christians, the "Agape" – the fellowship meal that often follows the Eucharistic service – is a celebration of this community. It too anticipates the Kingdom, which is to come.

To a very large extent our disunity as churches is due to our incapacity to practise this genuine sharing of gifts. One way of enriching our fellowship of sharing is by transforming the way we relate to each other as churches and as ecumenical organizations – a kind of horizontal sharing of the gifts of grace. Today, more than ever before, we need each other as churches. We must find new ways of deepening our fellowship as churches within the WCC fellowship. A new paradigm of being church to each other is an imperative in the 21st century work on ecumenical and ecclesial relationships. This is needed for the churches' self-empowerment, not for their own sake, but for the sake of each other and in order to gain the capacity to contribute to the world in dire need of better ways of relating.

I remember poor Indigenous women in Bolivia sharing the little they had after worship and creating a festive meal for everybody on the basis of the different varieties of potatoes they had brought to church. There, in that deprived community, the communal joy radiated as life met life in earnest. By sharing the little each had, the women did not become poorer than they had been; rather, they each became happier for each other because none went back home hungry. The miracle of feeding 5,000 (without counting women and children!) is a reality on a daily basis among the poor. Such celebrations of life among the poor remind me also of all the other parables of the invitation to the festive table that are told by Matthew, Mark, Luke and John in various ways. They all have in common that the host is deeply disappointed by the negative response of those invited in the first place. In an act of transformative justice, he extends the invitation to those from the streets and at the margins of society. They want to experience the healing power of the gospel in their daily lives. And this is for sure: they will celebrate with God when the usual patterns of exclusion and marginalization are turned upside down!

The *festa da vida* invites us to look afresh at the quality of our relationships and to put these relationships in the centre of the ecumenical movement. The Common Understanding and Vision (CUV) policy statement adopted at the Harare assembly called on WCC and its members to deepen their relationships with one another. To some extent, this has taken place, as in the important work of the Special Commission on Orthodox Participation in the World Council of Churches. We need to deepen our mutual accountability to one another, and do it in concrete and visible ways. The CUV also recognized that the ecumenical movement is broader than the World Council of Churches and called on it to develop its relationships with other Christian bodies, notably the evangelical and Pentecostal churches and other ecumenical organizations.

Our relationship with the Roman Catholic Church has matured over the years. The WCC and the Roman Catholic Church are very different bodies, but both are deeply committed to the ecumenical enterprise. For the last 40 years we have worked together fruitfully through the Joint Working Group. The WCC is grateful for the direct involvement of the Roman Catholic Church in our work to overcome the theological, historical and social divisions among the churches; in mission; in theological education; in the witness for justice in our world; in inter-religious dialogue; and in other ways. There is a natural tension between efforts towards deepening, and those towards widening, the fellowship of the churches constituting the WCC. This assembly gave an opportunity to re-focus attention on the quality of relationships within the fellowship, to explore together what it means to be in fellowship towards greater unity, and to challenge one another to manifest that unity more deeply. The assembly also reaffirmed our readiness to widen this fellowship through dialogue, inter-action and cooperation with sisters and brothers in Christ beyond the circle of membership in the WCC.

One concrete example is that of the Global Christian Forum, which brings together followers of Jesus Christ from a broader range of traditions and expressions than has ever been seen. The WCC is pledged to do everything in its power to continue to facilitate this encouraging process.

There is also a natural tension between the various institutional expressions of the ecumenical movement. All ecumenical organizations are struggling today with the question of how to respond to the changing ecclesial and ecumenical landscape. This is why we have begun to address together the major challenges to ecumenism in the 21st century – a process that goes beyond a narrow institutional focus that the term "re-configuration" might suggest. Just as there is the urgent need to work out mechanisms for coordinating our diakonia, advocacy and development, many actors in the ecumenical movement underline the need for defining together the common ecumenical vision and not only "the common vision of the WCC".

There are also some tensions in regard to inter-religious relationships. Many ask if this is integral to the ecumenical quest for Christian unity. We all recognize that we live in a multi-faith world, and we need to learn more about relating to people of other faiths, particularly at the community level. Beyond that, in addressing a broad range of world issues – and not just those involving conflicts between peoples of different religions – we need to learn how to relate, learn about the ways people of other faiths believe and see the world, and learn to act together for the good of our communities and of the world. Religion is increasingly recognized as playing a major role in international affairs, and we need to build relationships with other faith communities on all levels.

This was affirmed by the Critical Moment on Religious Dialogue Conference which the Council organized in June 2005. The meeting brought together participants from all major world religions in all parts of the world. One of the main conference recommendations was to call on the WCC to put in place mechanisms for bringing world religious leaders together to address jointly the problems facing the human community today. Inter-religious relationships should be given a high priority in the next period

The festival of life, to which we are all invited, is also an invitation to reach out to those we know and to those whom we don't yet know. We have long recognized that all of WCC's programmatic work is grounded in relationships and yet the reality is that different staff or teams are responsible for programme and for relationships. I hope for a more integrated and interactive approach to programme and relationships where our programmes strengthen the quality of our relationships and where our constituency feels more ownership of the programmes.

In what has been described as "the information age", our ecumenical movement is challenged to proclaim God's eternal Word and interpret its meaning across a wide range of cultures and technologies. As we seek creative ways to communicate, we remain committed to telling the love of Jesus, building trust and supporting the growth of base communities – both actual and virtual – in which spiritual fellowship may mature and lives may be transformed. The present context challenges us to re-think the following four current emphases of the ecumenical movement:

- **Faith and spirituality:** The central question of our time is the question of faith and the presence of Christ in the other. This is at the basis of our understanding of unity and mission. Faith must be central to our life together and must be the foundation for our ecumenical vision and engagement. What does Christian faith in the 21st century entail? This question is relevant to the Northern and Eastern churches as well as to the churches in the Global South. It is no longer a realistic expectation that

Christian faith formation takes place in the Christian families, in the churches and Sunday schools. At a time when issues of identity characterize political, social and interpersonal relationships, dialogue and cooperation between faiths become even more imperative.

- **Ecumenical formation:** This is one of those areas that surfaces forcefully, not merely as need or priority but as a real ecumenical imperative, as a determining factor that can have decisive influence on the ecumenical movement throughout the 21st century. In many member churches, a new generation of leadership seems not to be fully informed about the rich legacy and experience of the modern ecumenical movement. If contemporary Christians, including church leadership and staff, are to participate creatively and responsibly in the search for unity, and grow together, appropriate means of ecumenical formation must be offered to enable better, richer contributions to our common life. If we look at the Ecumenical Institute in Bossey, Switzerland, a model for ecumenical formation, we may discover two further challenges. First, in recent years, evangelicals and Pentecostals have been manifesting a clear interest in ecumenical courses and seminars, including programmes of graduate study. Second, young people have been pressing for more interreligious encounters and seminars.

- **Transformative justice:** In response to those who suffer the consequences of injustice that splits the world along the lines of poverty and wealth, work in the area of transformative justice is needed which integrates the care of creation, the transformation of unjust economic and social structures, a clear prophetic voice in global advocacy and prophetic diakonia. In the period since Harare, the WCC has explored the concept of transformative justice particularly in the area of overcoming racism. Instead of the more commonly used "restorative justice", the concept of transformative justice is based on the understanding that it is not possible to simply reinstate, re-establish, bring back, return – what has been lost. Transformative justice deals with the past in the present. Its goal is to overcome oppression and domination so as to achieve healing, reconciliation and the re-establish-ment ("to put things right") of people's relationships. My vision for the future is that we will explore this further as we continue to address issues of justice and diakonia, advocacy and dialogue. This will require creative new ways of addressing how the church's mission history has sometimes been interwoven with the breaking down of traditional forms of healing and reconciliation. It will include more direct processes of liberation and healing through encounter and dialogue between perpetrators of injustice and those who are victimized. This calls for a paradigm shift in our work, for *metanoia*, that will allow structures, culture, and defining values to be transformed. It will require us to re-direct our programmes towards more intentionally building truly inclusive and just com-munities which safeguard diversity, where different iden-tities and unity interact, and where the rights and obliga-tions of all are fully respected in love and fellowship. Transformative justice calls on the churches to make a costly commitment to overcome the divisions within their own life – our communities need to be transformed to live fully the diversity of their peoples and cultures as a clear reflection of God's creation and image in humankind. To be the church today is to be healing, reconciled and rec-onciling communities.

- **Being a moral voice to the world:** With growing recog-nition of the role of religion in public life, we have new opportunities to influence decisions on global policies. In fulfilling our historic responsibility we are challenged to become a strong, credible moral voice to the world: I hope that in the future we can develop fresh and creative ways of working which strengthen our relationships with churches and a wide range of ecumenical partners. These ways will take different forms with different partners. For example, I would like to see an interaction with Christian World Communions, especially those whose membership largely overlaps with the membership of the WCC, in our common commitment to visible unity and our common readiness to develop relationships with those churches and Christian families that do not actively participate in the ecumenical movement. I would like to see a closer programmatic relationship between WCC and the regional ecumenical organizations. I would like to see more intentional collaboration with international ecumenical organizations, which are often working on the same issues. I hope that initiatives to develop new ways of working in the field of development and diakonia with specialized ministries will bear fruit in the coming months and years.

But I want to go beyond these suggestions and renew the proposal that, as a concrete step, the next assembly of the WCC should provide a common platform for the wider ecumenical movement. If we are ready to take such a significant, concrete step we could envisage together, instead of the many different global assemblies and general conferences organized by the various world communions and other bodies, just one celebration of the search for unity and common witness of Christian churches. To be even more specific the WCC with the Lutheran World Federation and the World Alliance of Reformed Churches should explore possibilities of holding our next assemblies as a combined event. And we should also invite any other world Christian body to join us in this dialogue. This could be a means of beginning to plan together, so that we may even more effectively speak and act together.

The Word of God is a word of hope, the good news of transformation by grace. It is the proclamation of a new heaven and a new earth, where former things are no more. It is God's invitation to participate in a *festa da vida*, to rejoice in the feast of life! With God, all things are possible. And so we take up our responsibility, relying on God's transforming grace. All are welcome to the *festa da vida*; therefore, let us keep the feast! *

* This is an abridged version of the first report of Rev. Dr Samuel Kobia, general secretary, to the Ninth Assembly of the World Council of Churches at Porto Alegre, Brazil, 15 February, 2006.

1. An affair of the whole people of God

He has showed you what is good.
And what does the Lord require of you?
To act justly and to love mercy
and to walk humbly with your God.
Micah 6:8

This verse from the Old Testament has been a rallying cry for thousands of Christian social activists, especially among liberationists and those committed to changing unjust social structures. Micah prophesied in the eighth century (BCE) by issuing an indictment, an accusation, against the religious and secular leaders of Jerusalem. He pulled no punches. The indictment against the rulers and religious leaders is oppression of the poor, injustice and inequality, corruption and false institutional teaching. The threat is clear. Change your ways or Jerusalem will be a pile of ruins, the environment devastated. Then Micah tells the people that Yahweh has already told them what they should do. His focus, like that of all the prophets, was on this world, not another world. Micah was political, not just religious. He was passionate about justice in this world and about the destiny and fate of societies and peoples within history. Micah not only knew about God. He spoke as if he knew God. Terrible things were done to prophets who upset the institutions of their day. They were beaten, jailed, starved, humiliated and threatened with death because they challenged the rich and the powerful. They did not play it safe, they were not looking for security. The source of their courage was God.

Little known among mainline ecumenists today is something called the "Micah Challenge". It is a good example of the changing global ecumenical community made up of Pentecostals, evangelicals, some mainstream Protestants and even a few Roman Catholics trying to provide a new means for multi-country, international advocacy around the issues of global poverty and ecological destruction.

"Look at it another way," says Rev. Wesley Granberg-Michaelson, general secretary of the Reformed Church of America, "as our ecumenical institutions continue operating in present patterns, they become increasingly marginal in the global community. But we [the mainstream ecumenical movement] rarely make room for Pentecostals, evangelicals and Roman Catholics."

The Micah Challenge is an international grouping of Christians which aims to deepen Christian engagement with the poor and to influence leaders of rich and poor nations to fulfil their public promise to achieve the United Nations Millennium Development Goals (MDGs), and so halve global poverty by 2015.

All 191 member states of the UN promised in 2000 to achieve this. They include measurable, time-bound targets addressing poverty and hunger, education, maternal and child health, the prevalence of diseases including HIV and AIDS, gender equality, the environment, debt, trade justice and aid. The MDGs are achievable, but not unless people force governments to keep their promises.

The Micah Challenge was launched on October 15, 2004 in conjunction with the UN International Day for the Eradication of Poverty. It consists of 260 Christian community development organizations; the Challenge's purpose is to provide a means of multi-country, international advocacy around the issues of global poverty. This form of advocacy is, of course, not unique within agencies related to the ecumenical movement, but what is interesting is that it is a joint project with the World Evangelical Fellowship which has three million local churches in 111 countries with 120 national and regional evangelical church alliances, 104 organizational ministries and six specialized ministries. It is a worldwide church which is not connected with the institutionalized ecumenical movement, yet the Micah Challenge is facilitating a global campaign to mobilize Christians against poverty just as is the World Council of Churches and the wider ecumenical movement.

The Micah Network brings together more than 260 Christian organizations providing relief, development and justice ministries throughout the world. The majority are community development agencies in the South. The Micah Network aims to:

- strengthen the capacity of participating agencies to make a biblically-shaped response to the needs of the poor and oppressed;
- speak strongly and effectively regarding the nature of the mission of the Church to proclaim and demonstrate the love of Christ to a world in need; and
- prophetically influence the leaders and decision-makers of societies to maintain the rights of the poor and oppressed and rescue the weak and needy.

I use this example not to criticize but to illustrate our need for change. The future of the ecumenical movement is being challenged and overtaken – it is not eternal – by a radically redrawn map of Christianity. New configurations of the faith community will require a re-conceptualization of relationships so that in the future a Micah Challenge can be part of a new inclusive ecumenism, rather than being outside a protective institutionalism. The future must be shaped by a compelling spiritual vision rather than by predictable organizational momentum, and by deep change rather than the tiny steps of incremental change.

The ecumenical movement

The term "ecumenical" simply means the quest for visible Christian unity: a common witness through faith and order, mission and evangelism, service to the world (diakonia), and the promotion of justice and peace.

Before his crucifixion, Jesus prayed for his disciples and all Christians "that they may all be one, just as you, Father, are in me, and I in you, that they also may be in us, so that the world may believe that you have sent me" (John 17:21). Practically put, this means we are urgently called to transform our selfish and self-centred way of living into selfless love for each other and the society of which we are a part (the whole created world).

The world-wide ecumenical movement in the early years of the third millennium is a complex and complicated set of institutions which increasingly has great difficulties responding to Jesus' call to be one and to the changes demanded by the global situation in which we live in the 21st century. It is paralysed much of the time by institutionalism. It is no longer a living organism but a structure which has become instead of a means to an end, an end in itself.

As an example of the strictures placed on what was to have been a movement, ecumenism tries to carry out Jesus' exhortation through various and, in many cases, equally complex levels of ecumenical organizations such as the WCC itself, regional ecumenical organizations, sub-regional fellowships and national councils of churches. Layered onto these are the various world communions, each with its own hierarchies and bureaucracies, a plethora of mission agencies, ecumenical communities, theological colleges and associations, lay training centres, ecumenical development and advocacy agencies, emergencies operations, international organizations and many more.

The first testings of the WCC

It is very much like the United Nations and its hundreds of related agencies. Both were formed in the same year, 1948, both grew out of the appalling horrors of the second world war, both grew out of earlier international organizations. Both have large memberships with their own agendas and both are now widely seen as irrelevant to meeting the needs of a world which is bewilderingly different from the 20th century. A world constantly changing with a rapidity that institutions designed more than half a century ago cannot respond to with anything approaching dynamism and competence.

The first general secretary of the World Council of Churches, W.A. Visser 't Hooft, a Dutchman, once humorously remarked that the theology of the WCC was German, the financing was American and its bureaucracy was Dutch. Today, European churches are largely empty and their members growing older, American churches lack the funds and energy for the WCC and while the style of the bureaucracy remains stolidly old-fashioned European, the staff reflects the multi-racial, multi-cultural and multidenominational nature of the world. The point of Visser 't Hooft's comments, of course, is that the WCC, as the structure for the ecumenical movement of 1948, reflected the concerns of the world at that time which was predominantly northern and western and thoroughly acculturated to western European and American capitalism and their style of work.

Some, such as the revered theologian Karl Barth, fought bitterly against this profile, arguing that the ecumenical movement had but one mission and that was the prophetic mission of the poor and oppressed and that such things as neutrality were worse than irrelevant. In those years of the cold war, the institution was caught between member churches from the West and the East, between communism and capitalism (and their few surrogates in the Global South) and attempted to survive both ideologies by taking some kind of third path, then called "The Responsible Society."

The American churches, followed largely by the western Europeans, if somewhat less rhetorically, insisted bluntly that communism was the "greatest obstacle to world peace." Christians from the East saw communism as an anti-Fascist force which embodied much of the social concern for workers and oppressed races and classes which the church and "western civilization" should embody but had largely lost. The WCC, with its feet firmly planted on both sides of the divide, came out with a statement which said: "The churches should reject both the ideologies of communism and capitalism and should draw men [sic] from the false assumption that these extremes are the only alternatives." The real significance of this statement made during the first assembly at Amsterdam in 1948 was that the WCC refused to identify itself with any political or social ideology and was able in many concrete ways to bridge the polarization of the cold war. The term "Responsible Society" provided a signpost for social justice and action.

However, as in the UN, these carefully neutral statements, however nuanced, created the impression in more politicized churches that the ecumenical movement was identified with the West and capitalism or, as the cold war solidified during the 1950s, that the WCC was soft on communism as it opened its membership to Eastern Orthodox churches in Russia and the Warsaw Pact nations. The fellowship of the WCC was in serious danger of being fractured.

Was the ecumenical movement to be stillborn? Was its duty to maintain at all cost its community with its member churches, no matter their own ideologies? Or was it to render concrete witness regarding the critical issues of international life such as the impending Korean War, the independence of colonial states in Africa and Asia and the nuclear threat between the US and the USSR? The third world war was thought by many to be simply a matter of time, a short time.

The WCC again refused to take sides but said its clear duty was both to relationships with member churches and to address the crucial issues of the world. "It would be a true ecumenical disaster if the day were to come that all interchurch relations across the dividing line of East and West were broken," Visser 't Hooft wrote to the Executive Committee in 1951 as the Korean War was raging, involving China, the USSR, the US, the two Koreas and the UN.

"But it is also essential the World Council continue to speak to the churches concerning the perilous issues of our time. A World Council which would cease to struggle for a concrete witness would soon become irrelevant and therefore also cease to create real fellowship. And in the situation in which we find ourselves today, in which men and women in their deep uncertainty and confusion long for a word of guidance from a truly ecumenical, world-embracing perspective, it would be a very serious matter to give up our attempts to find and speak such a word."

Throughout the last half of the 20th century and the cold war, the WCC continued to try to find and speak that word. It paid dearly in terms of controversy for its positions during the deliberate mass starvation of people in Biafra (Eastern Nigeria) in 1968-70 and its long struggle against apartheid in South Africa in the Programme to Combat Racism (PCR).

Long before it became fashionable, the ecumenical movement saw God's Created Order as inclusive of all species and all living things and headed into advocating for the environment. Liberation movements were supported in Africa, liberation theology came from Latin America and the revolutions against military dictatorships and civilian autocrats occupied a large place in the WCC agendas, along with a new more equal role for women in the life of the churches. It seemed there was not an issue across the globe about which the WCC did not have a resolution or a committee, sub-committee, working group, conference, task force or ad hoc meeting.

And the institution grew larger and more diverse but also ever-more structured, and restructured. Meetings were held all over the world and in Geneva almost every day until finally, in what to some seemed the ultimate in absurdity, two separate weeks a year were set aside just for the meetings for staff. People who were connected to the WCC were often referred to as the "Ecumenical Jet Set".

Fifty years after Amsterdam, the last assembly of the 20th century was held in Harare, Zimbabwe and a Golden Jubilee was celebrated. Poignantly, but unsurprisingly, the highlight of the 10-day meeting attended by some 5,000 people from all over the planet was a look-back to the Council's heydays in the three-hour Jubilee celebration.

Journey to Jubilee featured two octogenarians and a septuagenarian who took the wildly-cheering participants through 50 years of churches together in the WCC with high-tech large-screen video presentations from Amsterdam to Harare. Former South African President Nelson Mandela and former WCC general secretary Philip Potter gave fervent and poignant testimonies of the churches' common witness in society and looked forward to a Centennial in 2048. Pauline Webb, veteran BBC broadcaster and the first woman to be elected a vice-moderator of the WCC Central Committee, who hosted the show, murmured to a friend: "I wonder if, like the UN, we have reached our 'sell by…' date."

In the midst of ringing endorsements of solidarity with Africa and the role of women in the churches, the eighth assembly was clearly aware that all was not well in the official ecumenical world. It issued a major policy statement in 1998 called *Towards a Common Understanding and Vision of the World Council of Churches* (ever after to be known by its acronym, CUV) and set up a *Special Commission on Orthodox Participation in the World Council of Churches* which reported its findings in 2004. Both actions pointed to serious problems which needed to be wrestled with: what have the churches learned in 50 years of ecumenical history in the WCC? What are the implications of what has been learned? How should we as churches respond as we look into the daunting and constantly changing third millennium? CUV was meant to guide that reflection. The Special Commission was set in a context of ominous rumblings of discontent and two outright withdrawals of Eastern Orthodox churches.

The WCC at 50 was both venerable and vulnerable.

Times of change

The challenges of living and working in a world of extremes that is constantly changing have been described and analyzed even as the changes catch up and pass by the analysis. It is a world unimaginable to the founders of the WCC and the ecumenical movement.

Nonetheless, in its principal features, it is a world ever more dangerous, and just as polarized, as the one which faced ecumenists after the end of the second world war only now it is a global world we know about instantaneously. It is dominated by concentrations of wealth and power walled in beside masses of horrible poverty, disease and war.

It is a world of brilliant new technologies and mind-expanding access to information for people living in the midst of earth-shattering climate change and global warming that pose a definite threat of extinction. All Creation is endangered, even as science and technology experiment with manipulation of life processes.

There is a sense of violence let loose that the post-second world war international order centred on the UN and its agencies, can no longer control. Instead we find the oppressive process of economic and financial globalization, reinforced now since 11 September 2001, through the open defiance of international law by the George W. Bush administration in the US intent on pursuing a hegemonic unilateralism, building on its crushing military and economic superiority. The "war on terror" has engulfed many areas of the world and created a fearful sense of threat to Muslims wherever they live that they are responsible for violence simply because of their beliefs. Extremism knows no boundaries of faith.

As tensions rise to the breaking point between peoples of different religions, the ecumenical vision must change radically. It is precisely on the question of how Christians relate to people of other faiths and no faith that we currently require urgently a new round of multilateral theological engagement. As Christians, as churches, we should be inquiring together as to what is God's purpose for us in a multi-cultural world characterized by a diversity of faiths.

The agenda of Visser 't Hooft and his successors has changed dramatically but the ecumenical movement has not. The CUV recognized this back in the previous millennium: "The WCC as an institution must not be paralysed by institutionalism, for its vocation in the service of the churches and the ecumenical movement requires that it be a living organism, responding to new challenges brought by changing times, new ecumenical partners and growing discernment of the ecumenical calling."

Konrad Raiser, the former WCC general secretary, claimed that what the WCC is often criticized for, is also valid for the other ecumenical partners who have developed "elaborate institutional structures and procedures accompanied by a high degree of professionalization of their activities." Many follow bureaucratic models similar to the UN and its agencies, governments and civil service; others have taken to the style of multi-national corporations; and still others try to become like NGOs. But in whatever model, the dynamism, vision and prophetic voice that once characterized the ecumenical movement has been subjected to a plethora of strict bureaucratic demands which are rigorously reinforced by the requirements of representation (membership in various denominations, geographic sectors, gender, and minorities), high salaries and benefits leading to financial crises, restructuring, downsizing and consequent low staff morale.

Along with these almost incomprehensible layers of structures, the ecumenical movement also contains a wide variety of networks, non-governmental organizations, coalitions, initiatives and campaigns all connected in some way with institutional churches, usually around specific issues. Raiser called this the "movement" dimension of ecumenism, i.e. "they are flexible, limited in institutional arrangements and essentially based on personal commitment. They are heavily dependent on leadership figures and make maximum use of modern, electronic means of communications."

While there is some sense of competition and even antagonism between the institutional and movement dimensions, each represents complementary aspects of ecumenism. What is of concern is that institutional constraints are so dominant that innovative and critical voices and initiatives have become marginalized.

These two dimensions of the churches have existed for a very long time as a kind of "double face" of institution and movement. Institutionally this is characterized by an ordered life, recognition of authority, an ordained ministry and official teachings. As movements, most churches have developed specialized ministries which respond to various needs and challenges, especially in the areas of mission, service and formation. Often they have their own structures and leadership and try to maintain as much independence as possible in their work. Whereas the institutional life of these historic churches (Christian World Communions among them) is mainly concerned with maintaining the integrity of the churches' internal life, specialized ministries for mission, service and diakonia (service) are directed outwards towards the "world". These different dimensions between the institutional churches and specialized ministries have emerged in many of the large historic churches of the West but do not apply in the same way to the burgeoning newer churches of the South, nor to the Eastern and Oriental Orthodox churches.

The ecumenical movement through the WCC has tried from its beginning in 1948 (and earlier) to keep these two faces of the life of the church together. Raiser says this reflects the "conviction that mission, service and diakonia belong to the *being* of the church and not only to its *activities*." However, despite the successes of linking mission to the institutional church, there is a growing separation of church and service ministries. The latter follows different criteria than those applied in organized churches, placing the WCC under severe stress at the beginning of the 21st century and contributing to a sense of fragmentation and a lack of focus and coherence.

The majority of the historic churches place their primary ecumenical emphasis on the search for "visible unity" or as some call it, "churchly ecumenism". This was the central focus of the Special Commission and, within the Roman Catholic Church, the various bilateral dialogues with church families (i.e. Anglican, Lutheran, Orthodox, Reformed, etc.). Indeed, the CUV document describes this orientation of the Council as the "fellowship of churches on the way towards full *koinonia*".

However, a realistic assessment of the churches shows that most of them, institutionally speaking, are more concerned with maintaining and defending their own identity than with strengthening unity. Indeed, the retiring Moderator of the Central Committee said in a speech in New York in 2005 that institutional ecumenism was in "stagnation". His Holiness Aram I, patriarch of the Armenian Apostolic Church (Cilicia) told a special symposium on the future of the ecumenical movement in the 21st century that "a new identity and a new self-understanding" was needed if the movement was to move beyond institutional ecumenism and become "a healing reality". Aram added that "to be church means being ecumenical but it can no longer be a private club for conference-goers and church hierarchs".

It seems the time has come to recognize that the ecumenical movement and agenda have outgrown the institutionalized churches and that councils and structures set up to meet the needs of the particular moment – such as the crisis at the end of the second world war or apartheid in South Africa – are not eternal, not even the World Council of Churches is eternal. Some say that the ecumenical movement is too precious to be left to the churches and their leaders alone!

But this great problem facing the ecumenical movement seems built into its very essence. David Gill, an Australian veteran of the ecumenical movement, wrote several decades ago that "the notion of churches, having demonstrated that their hearts are in the right place by joining an ecumenical body, can now leave ecumenism to the World Council and get on with denominational business-as-usual." The WCC is seen as an instrument for protecting denominational prerogatives. Indeed, denominations seem to some a barrier of protection against clarifying and reaffirming the essential and exhilarating ecumenical vision, which is their oneness in Christ. Instead many prefer an ecumenism of the status quo.

"The ecumenical movement is an affair of the whole people of God and it must regain its original vocation of being a renewal movement of and in the churches. The heavy institutionalization of church life corresponds less and less to the actual needs of the people," Raiser wrote in 2003 for a Geneva round table on reconfiguring the ecumenical movement.

"The search for visible unity needs new priorities. It needs to be the search for life in true community, especially at the local level, as is manifested by the enormous growth of Pentecostal and evangelical communities everywhere. Councils of churches have become too clerical, too dependent on leaders ordained by member churches and have lost the energy provided by active lay people including students, youth and women's fellowships."

Multilateralism

After the Harare assembly in 1998, the WCC increasingly was pushed to realize and admit that its role of furthering the coherence of the one ecumenical movement was being frustrated by its mode of governance. It had to accept the reality of the separation between the institutional churches and their specialized ministries. Mere membership, which had been the criteria so far for participation, was no longer appropriate. Church-related partner agencies, specialized ministries, networks and movements contribute substantial funds, receive lengthy reports but are not part of the Council's planning and decision-making. A better way must be found to allow the WCC to act as intermediary – along with regional ecumenical organizations – to connect, analyze, interpret and provide the space necessary to agree on priorities for action. The implementation of this ecumenical action will lie with partners on different levels. But, partner agencies are only one component of the ecumenical movement.

On the ground, at the local levels and especially in the South, new movements of Christian people spring up constantly and do not fit easily with existing structures and frameworks. New non-denominational communities are emerging everywhere from inner city London to the fetid slums of Nairobi and the ramshackle *favelas* of Rio de Janeiro. At the same time, denominationalism seems on the increase in the traditional churches of the ecumenical movement. Coalitions around justice and environmental issues, for example, move out of, and around, existing local and national councils of churches, often even in cooperation with other faiths and secular agencies. The scene is in a constant state of movement and flux. The highly-institutionalized ecumenical organizations have great difficulty relating to these local manifestations of ecumenism. Inter-church and interfaith coalitions are often the best way of working and they include churches, such as the Roman Catholics or Pentecostals, who are not even members of WCC. And they are effective agents of change. But others worry that this leads to fragmentation and disunity, even chaos. The new and always-changing situation early in the 21st century calls more and more for a reaffirmation of a multilateralism that is open for new partners. One model of interest is the World

Social Forum (WSF) which began in 2001 at Porto Alegre, Brazil, the site of the WCC's assembly in 2006. The WSF theme is "Another World is Possible."

According to its charter of principles, the WSF is not an organization, not even a united front platform, but "...an open meeting place for reflective thinking, democratic debate of ideas, formulation of proposals, free exchange of experiences and inter-linking for effective action, by groups and movements of civil society that are opposed to neo-liberalism and to domination of the world by capital and any form of imperialism, and are committed to building a society centred on the human person."

It is a statement of multilateralism which the ecumenical movement might well wish to pay serious attention to, given its global nature and that many church-related groups are involved in WSF activities. And, to further multilateralism within all conciliar bodies at all levels is a major, urgent task in which the WCC, charged with maintaining the coherence of the ecumenical movement, must play a key role. It is a long-term programme which the Porto Alegre assembly mandated for a new ecumenical configuration with simplified and flexible structures of governance.

There are other participants in ecumenical ventures who put primary emphasis on Christian diversity. The goal of this movement, however, is not so much to unite diversity as to recognize the proper diversity of our God-given oneness. Perhaps the best way to underscore this is by stressing that "Christian" is the noun that primarily defines all who are in Christ. "We are black Christians and white Christians and are, therefore, related at a level deeper than race. We are female Christians and male Christians and are, therefore, related at a level deeper than gender. We are liberal Christians and conservative Christians and are, therefore, related at a level deeper than ideology. We are North American and Western European Christians and African and Asian and Latin American Christians and are, therefore related at levels deeper than nationality or region or continent." (*Councils of Churches and the Ecumenical Vision*, Kessler and Kinnamon, WCC, 2000.)

The important question to be resolved is how a more coherent, dynamic, focused and responsive configuration of the ecumenical movement would emerge. Obviously, opportunities must be created for all expressions of the ecumenical mandate to come together and to engage in common planning. Suggestions that, as a first step, the next assemblies of the Lutheran World Federation (LWF), the World Alliance of Reformed Churches (WARC) and the WCC meet together were approved by the ninth WCC assembly this year. This proposal, while complex, could be seen as a first step towards a comprehensive gathering of all who are part of the ecumenical movement. Some preliminary testing for reconfiguration has already begun in the African context by the All Africa Conference of Churches (AACC) based in Nairobi.

The three classical elements of the ecumenical movement's streams – unity, mission and justice and service – could serve as the basis for a fellowship of churches using models such as the Canadian coalitions which bring denominations (including Roman Catholics and some evangelicals) together around social justice issues. Other examples could be the specialized organizations within the system of the UN. Raiser has talked about a "federalist system" using three interlocking functional circles representing classical focuses of unity, mission and justice and service. Within the circle of unity, the traditional denominations and new movements could be linked. In the mission circle would be mission boards and communities of Christians. The specialized ministries of development, advocacy and diakonia could meet in the third circle on justice and service.

The more important question in analyzing the interlocking circles concept of the early days of this century is whether a coherent, dynamic and responsive configuration of the ecumenical movement would emerge. Obviously new models of governance would need to be developed. All expressions of ecumenism would have to come together for exchange and planning. Perhaps the next assembly of the WCC could be transformed into such an occasion.

Global Christian Forum

The vision of the Global Christian Forum (GCF) includes the WCC. The GCF met first at Fuller Theological Seminary in Pasadena, CA, in 2000, and its vision is simple but bold: can the four main "families" of the Christian community – Orthodox, historic Protestant, evangelical and Pentecostal, and Roman Catholic – be brought into intentional, ongoing fellowship on the global level?

At the first meeting, 30 representatives of a variety of Christian traditions including the WCC, tried to come forward with ideas for a forum of Christian churches and ecumenical organizations that goes "beyond the present ecumenical structures as a step forward in the efforts to bring the various expressions of today's Christianity around the common table for dialogue and cooperation."

This Forum includes most of what could be called the ecumenical stakeholders, many of whom are not part of the WCC, such as the Roman Catholics who, despite a 40-year history of work with the WCC, will not join, believing they are a single church and not a denomination. The Orthodox and certain conservative evangelical groups criticize the WCC for having been "hi-jacked by European and North American liberals". As well as representatives from these churches, Christian networks and para-church organizations attended.

According to the official communiqué, "Although the idea of such a Forum originally arose in conversations within the WCC, the development of the proposals is now under the leadership of an independent continuation committee. The discussions at the meeting explored ways to go beyond the present ecumenical structures so that churches from a wider range of traditions may have a common space to discuss issues of mutual concern."

For several years this fragile initiative has worked with scarce funding and minimal recognition, but has begun producing promising fruit. An example is found in regional consultations of the GCF, the first of which was in Asia in May 2004. A member of the Evangelical Fellowship of India, Richard Howell, said the Global Christian Forum "is the best thing that could have happened to the Christian church in Asia. It created an open space where people could come together for the first time to share their stories and faith journey." He spoke vigorously about the growth of Christianity in Asia: "...growth brings challenges. The Global Christian Forum gave an opportunity for those from different traditions to listen. We discovered one another. And we discovered Christ at work within our different traditions."

In August, 2005 the GCF held its African regional consultation in Lusaka, Zambia. About 70 church leaders from all parts of Africa, including Baptist, Anglican, Pentecostal, Reformed, Roman Catholic, Orthodox, Seventh Day Adventist, evangelical, and Lutheran churches, as well as the AACC, the Association of Evangelicals in Africa, the International Fellowship of Evangelical Students, the World Student Christian Federation, World Vision, the United Bible Societies, the African Theological Fellowship, various national councils of churches, and the African Instituted Churches, participated.

Why was this so important? Simply because it had never happened before. As Ekow Badu Wood of the Ghana Pentecostal Council put it: "this has been a beautiful opportunity for churches that have been marginalized to be given the opportunity to speak."

Assembly landmark event

And so the ninth assembly of the WCC, as the most comprehensive and representative global ecumenical organization in modern Christianity, met for the first time in the third millennium at Porto Alegre to begin an urgent and critical new phase in the search for Christian unity. WCC assemblies have been landmark events in the life of the ecumenical movement for almost 60 years, gathering together a unique and comprehensive spectrum of Christians and churches characterized by their vision of a new culture and forms for the modern ecumenical movement.

The assembly was held in the midst of widespread injustice, poverty and despair. The immense challenges which face humankind call for careful and wise discernment of the "signs of the times", and courageous visions of hope from the ecumenical movement. The 4,000 or so participants were well aware that the assembly was speaking to a world in need of profound transformation, as the prayerful theme suggested: "God, in your grace, transform the world."

We live in an era marked by destructive power and disgraced human dignity. Economic and cultural globalization, new forms of militarism and domination, and ecological destruction have never been so evident. The prevailing international economic and political models have failed to stem the tide of injustice and inequality.

The religious context is evolving just as rapidly as the secular, and religious identity has returned to the public sphere in a stunning variety of ways that give the lie to those who thought religion had been overcome by technology. While the 20th century was dominated by confrontations between ideologies, "identity" is emerging as one of the most characteristic and divisive features of the 21st century. All Christians are being challenged to look at their identity in the context of a new religious plurality.

The theme of the assembly was both a prayer and a hope. It reminds us that God, in Christ, has offered humankind and the whole creation reconciliation and new life. Thus the assembly was designed to give urgency and energy towards a renewed ecumenical agenda for the 21st century, one which will be as crucial as was the first assembly of the second millennium which faced a world near collapse. The transformation of the world is being presented as a new challenge to the ecumenical movement.

Against the background of continuing conflicts in Iraq and Afghanistan, the threats against Iran, violence and broken peace accords in Palestine and Israel, genocide in Darfur, Sudan and, perhaps above all, the fearsome and misnamed war on terror, the assembly marked the completion of the first five years of the Decade to Overcome Violence (DOV) as a way of mobilizing the churches' peace-making efforts and resources. The question for the churches remains: how can we together foster a culture of peace, seeking to restore the authentic nature of our humanity, in a context where violence has become so accepted and pervasive?

At Harare in 1998, the WCC and the ecumenical movement made a commitment to walk in solidarity with Africa. Yet, entire regions of the continent face poverty, famine, disease and war. Two particular areas are of special concern for the future.

The presence and participation of young people were visible and substantial throughout the assembly, although our institutional rules still make their aspirations and interests difficult to hear. Their involvement was frustrated by our forms of governance so this emphasis on bringing youth into the centre must continue well beyond Porto Alegre as a matter of high priority. The ecumenical movement will have to take spirituality much more seriously in order to nourish and more fully undergird our ecumenical experience together.

The WCC is, first and foremost, a fellowship of churches. In recent years, we have consistently stated our desire to both deepen and broaden this fellowship. Following the Special Commission on Orthodox Participation, the adoption of a consensus model of decision-making and its use at Porto Alegre deepened the sense of fellowship and assisted with the difficult questions with discernment.

It became clear at Porto Alegre that the stifling nature of the WCC's proliferation of structures at all levels was not only unsustainable but is a barrier to recapturing the vision, dynamism and sense of an ecumenical *movement*. This diverts human and material resources away from ecumenical activities in the churches and society into the maintenance of overlapping and badly outmoded structures. It is absolutely essential that a radically new approach to ecumenism in the 21st century must seriously and urgently change its configurations.

While promoting visible Christian unity remains the core mission of the Council, the Porto Alegre assembly gave impetus to new forms of work and it became clear that the WCC should do less but do it better. Proliferation was not only a barrier to ecumenism, the WCC also had to raise its level of dynamism and willingness to implement radical change in its structures and forms of governance if its future service to the ecumenical movement is to survive.

It is increasingly clear that the ecumenical movement has reached an important point of transition, and that new categories of activity may be needed. The Council will engage in less programmatic activities, but must deepen its involvement in strategic areas. We have to find new ways of relating to and communicating with our member churches and ecumenical partners and move towards a more integrated, interactive and dynamic way of working as a movement.

There is not only a real potential of the churches together to contribute to the transformation of the world, in spite of the reality of the difficulties we face, there is also a biblical imperative that we must change to be faithful.

In the spirit of John 17:21 "that all of them may be one … so that the world may believe that you have sent me" and because of our common faith in a reconciling God (II Cor. 5:18-21), we intend:

- to deepen our commitment to God's mission in the world;
- to enhance our understanding of contemporary expressions of Christian mission (Matt. 28:19,20, Matt. 22: 37-39, John 20:21 and Acts 1:8);
- to pursue principles and practices that would enable us to handle our Christian differences and distinctiveness creatively and peaceably;
- to engage in theological reflection in areas of common concern;
- to strengthen the wholeness of the church by encouraging communication and cooperation; and
- to foster relationships that may lead to common witness. (GCF, 2000)

It was within this history and context that I began to travel, listen and dialogue with Christians around the world to try and understand and help to implement a vision that could deepen and broaden the ecumenical movement.

2. The voices of the people

I believe that if we are to find an idea equal to our perilous times, it is this; that the one God, creator of diversity, commands us to honour Creation by respecting diversity. Some will view this as a departure from the premise which inspired the founders of the ecumenical movement: "that they all may be one". Perhaps in some ways it is, but I believe it is also fundamentally a part of Jesus' prayer and this is where the process of reconfiguration will lead us. *

The future of ecumenism depends on how willing we are to recognize that there is dignity in diversity and difference. The biggest challenge to the ecumenical movement is how to see, define and make diversity and unity visible in all our expressions of faith. There are four trends we can see in our globalized world, the one based on neo-liberal economic theory which threatens to undermine the very diversity upon which unity is premised:

Identity: We are now in a time when the peoples of the world are experiencing a mighty turning of history and culture, a time of change, confusion, anxiety, opportunity, and hope. Social forces (mobility, technology, population growth, media, commerce, etc.) are pulling us together, both as individuals and societies, as they are also pushing us apart. This double possibility – of union and differentiation – is, in relation to human identity, the great challenge of our time. We are thus faced with the need to discover new ways of defining our identity in relation to self and others. Is the whole of humanity in an "identity crisis"? If so, what are the roots of this crisis and how is it manifested in the world? How is the human self-definition changing?

Being in transition: The world situation today is highly pressurized and tensions are volatile. During transition periods, old patterns disintegrate as new patterns of behaviour, thought, and communication become established. Conflicts and tensions often arise when representatives of the old order find themselves challenged by those whose lives are

* Rev. D. Samuel Kobia, with the Pacific Conference of Churches, the leaders of Pacific churches and the Episcopal Conference of the Pacific (Roman Catholic) Suva, Fiji, 2004.

committed to bringing the new order into being. Pressure mounts as these interests grow increasingly polarized, until the need for release from the tension becomes paramount. Our need for a positive explanation that makes sense of these times is exceeded only by our need to weather the changes gracefully, without reactivity. Religions traditionally offered such wisdom and challenge. Yet, the disparity of belief systems results in fragmentation and often works against the common good. How can we encourage religious leaders to move beyond concern for their specific congregations or faith communities into a caring for the whole of humanity?

Notions of truth: In those worldviews shaped by the influence of monotheism and western philosophy in general, there has been a dominating desire for truth. That is, a belief in a core reality which shapes reality and all of life. A belief in and desire for truth has driven much of the intellectual life in the cultures dominated by these worldviews. Various ways of defining truth have shaped the nature of cultural, ethnic, religious, and social self-definitions. The belief in truth has provided both a base for morality and a base for defining what is worth dying or killing for in order to protect. In these days dominated by a belief in the rhetoric of truth, we might well consider a few central questions. How do current notions of truth define the lines of opposition between competing truths? Is it possible to have dialogue across truths? If so, how can this dialogue be encouraged?

Trustworthiness: Doubts regarding the trustworthiness of humankind surround the paradox of our capacity for extreme, opposing acts, both on an individual and group level. Centuries of wars and intentional cruelties are juxtaposed with acts of great love, self-sacrifice, and caring. We need a vision of human trustworthiness that is both realistic and positive. Now is the time to work towards imagining and creating such a vision. Is there widespread scepticism regarding humankind's trustworthiness? If so, what are the antecedents for this distrust? How does the essential need for meaning and worth in one's community contribute to or undermine the sense of trust? How can persons caught in social, ethnic and religious conflict learn to trust their opponents and be grateful for their opposition? How do our notions of good and evil inhibit our ability to appreciate and trust the humanness in all people? What factors do we already know, and what are those we can imagine, that can transform the devastating psychological and spiritual aftermaths of wars and violence into reconciliation and forgiveness? How can we generate a positive vision of human trustworthiness?

Community: The desire for community, and by extension union, is basic to the human condition. This urge is heightened in contemporary times by our unpreparedness to negotiate as a species the often-perilous byways of interior and external life. We are only beginning to understand the deepest implications regarding this basic human need and the necessity for literacy of self, other, and culture. Can the unified state be defined in ways that allow the full range of diversity to be expressed? If so, how might this be done? Spiritual union is generally thought to require some form of "death". Can the expectation of death or apocalyptic disaster be understood in ways that do not generate fear? If so, how might this be accomplished? In what ways do we deny our desires for and fear of community?

Since the latter part of the 20th century and now in the first decade of the 21st massive changes and reconfigurations in economics and politics have forced the ecumenical movement to address global issues in order to be ready to provide leadership in the goals set out above:

- Neo-liberal economic theory (globalization) offers enhanced wealth creation at a rate higher than at any time in human history for a relative few but at a cost too high for the masses to pay. It undermines the very diversity upon which our unity and solidarity are premised. Apart from the abhorrent poverty and deprivation for millions all over the world, environmental degradation and the shameless amassing of wealth for a few, there is such violent instability that arms merchants (among them, the most prolific sales are made to the poorest areas by the five permanent members of the UN) constantly proliferate. But the most frightening issue is that globalization homogenizes diverse cultural societies regardless of historical and cultural conditions. Their message is stark: "if our way of conducting economic activities is right, then yours is wrong". Daily the mantras from the West are repeated: "globalization is inevitable"; and from the South: "we will be left out if we do not join".

- The interdependence resulting from globalization is so pervasive that a negative trend results, reversing what is familiar both in terms of cultural and religious beliefs. Sovereign nation states, particularly in the Global South, are caught between a future that lacks direction as a result of the decentralization of power and the increasingly uncertain abilities to apply the rule of law and a present, on the other hand that is highly unstable for them in terms of sovereignty and identity. In the ecumenical movement this is especially paralysing because confessional churches (denominations) are intimately tied to cultural and traditional structures and expectations. The most alluring option left then, is for us to revert back to older beliefs and become legalistic in our interpretation and application of biblical and faith beliefs. In such a situation, can extremism and fundamentalism be far behind?

- Church-state relations have reconfigured themselves dramatically in this century around the much-misunderstood global terrorism, especially in the US since 11 September 2001. Fundamentalism in a wide variety of forms is proliferating, advocating through television and the internet especially, a "Christian" hatred of other religions – very particularly Islam – and other expressions of Church – especially those alleged to be liberal. Their growth and closeness to the administration of the US tipped church-state relations in favour of extremism and fundamentalism. It also excluded non-fundamentalist Christian denominations and movements as moral voices resisting war and violent conflict, abrogation of human rights, corruption and amassing of wealth for the military-industrial complex while raising questions about poverty, inequality, racism and extreme religious intolerance. What response or choice do the churches and movements of the WCC have in this configuration? Do we align ourselves with fundamentalism which might appear the line of least resistance or do we step back and assess where we can make the most impact. These may not be easy choices but we are not called to take the easy road, the pragmatic decision.

- The prescription advanced by international financial institutions and the powerful militarized West, that free market democracy is the only path for the entire world, forces developing countries to adopt this highly questionable and immoral ideology if they are to achieve the western world's level of development. If developing countries and economies wish to participate in the "free" market they have no choice but to accept the rawest form of western-style democracy. The fact that there is a gigantic abyss between the principles of the so-called free market and the democracy touted by the US is irrelevant. For most developing countries the result is highly visible. If they reject globalization, they are marginalized out of existence. If they embrace it, tensions and conflicts spring up across the South over identities, resources, concentration of wealth and conflicts along ethnic and religious lines.

It seems clear that people living in a world of enormous transition who yearn for identity, truth, trustworthiness and community regardless of their faith allegiance find these 21st century global trends a direct challenge to their hopes and aspirations. By undermining differences and diversity, we risk a perilous future. When ecumenism fails to recognize that diversity is God's Creation then we view differences as a barrier to genuine development. Ever since biblical times – the Babylonian, Egyptian and Roman eras – human history has been blighted by attempts to do away with diversity at a great cost to human life, cultures and the environment.

We thought that the way to unity and prosperity was to impose one culture, one tradition and one belief system upon all other communities. That is why human history, despite gains and advances, is sadly marred by brutality, oppression and the reduction of differences to mere problems to be solved. That is why, perhaps more than ever before, our challenge is to determine how to perceive and appreciate diversity and how it is utterly essential for our unity.

For almost 60 years the ecumenical movement has made "the visible unity" of the churches its biblical-based mantra. But, somehow this was too often translated into uniformity, much as globalization, wrongly, translates capitalism into democracy.

The challenge of the ecumenical family in this new millennium then, is the legitimization of diversity – an enormous task and a paradigm shift – which means the reconfiguration of our theological basis, our liturgical expression and our institutional expression. To achieve unity we need to work for, and sustain in reality, diversity. The ecumenical movement must be a counterbalance to the idea that one God must mean one faith, one truth, one covenant.

The first 11 chapters of Genesis tell the story of a universal project of one language, one religion, one culture. It ended, as it was bound to, in the Tower of Babel – a project which demonically underpins much of what we see in the world today. This passage (Genesis 11:1-9) tells how Babel was a tower built by a united humanity to reach the heavens. Because humans had it in their heart to be like God, the Creator stopped the project by confusing their speech so that each spoke a different language. As a result, they could no longer communicate with one another and the work was halted. The builders were then scattered to different parts of the Earth.

This relates to the fading dream of a Christian (and northern) hegemony and the growing challenge to recognize cultural and religious plurality as Jesus did during his life on earth. He ate meals with all kinds of people, going far beyond the limits of his class, culture and religion. He was open to women, children, prostitutes, lepers, the mentally ill, Samaritans, Romans (all the people his religion despised) and let a Syrio-Phoenician woman remind him that he must open his heart to those of other traditions. Jesus did not tell the woman to be converted so as to benefit from his ministry, but affirmed her difference and recognized her faith.

Today, in a world which lives in proximity to difference more than ever before, we need to understand that:

- Just as the natural environment depends on biodiversity,

- So does the human environment depend on cultural and religious diversity; and

- Because no one creed has a monopoly on spiritual truth,

- No one civilization encompasses all spiritual, ethical and artistic expressions of humanity.

Diversity will shape the expressions and forms of confessional faiths

While we have come a long way in the past century in recognizing God in the confessional faiths of each other, we have much further to go in recognizing God in others. This to many may seem a word-game but its implications are profound and radical, especially in our institutions and structures:

- Can we recognize the image of God in those whose language, faith and ideals are different from ours?

- Can we recognize the image of God in the young and elderly among us, and their quest for meanings which are at odds with our articles of faith?

- Can we recognize the image of God in the poor, oppressed and marginalized of our community?

To grapple specifically and intentionally with these profound questions will be deeply painful for many. The hope lies in covenant, a concept that must be at the centre of things as we try to shape the ecumenism of the future. Two points about covenant:

1. Covenant affirms diversity and the dignity of difference. The great covenant relationships between God and Creation, between people in marriage, between members of a community or citizens of a society exist because all parties to the covenant recognize that "it is not good for man to be alone". God cannot redeem the world without human participation, any more than humans can redeem the world without God. Covenants exist because we are different and seek to preserve that difference, even as we come together with our huge variety of gifts for the common good. The very recognition that difference is a source of blessing leads us to conflict resolution, mediation, conciliation, peace and unity – unity based on diversity not uniformity, union based on freedom, not uniformity, a unity based on freedom, not regulation.

2. Covenants, because they are relational, not rational and logical, are also pluralistic. A person has a different relationship with parents, spouses, children, friends, neighbours, faith community members and citizens, but none of these is exclusive. Denominational or confessional faith, covenant tells us, is a form of relationship with God and that one relationship does not exclude the other. Nowhere is this more explicit than in the great prophet Isaiah-vision of the time when the two historical enemies of Israel – Egypt and Assyria – will one day become God's chosen people alongside Israel itself.

Listening amid the din of dissonant dominant voices

We seem to have lost some of the spirit that has led us to take risks in the past. Our organizational structures have seemed instead to be embroiled in the task of taking care of internal, institutional and programmatic survival between assemblies. Self-preservation has become our preoccupation, and through an inwardly-directed obsession with our own structures we have lost the space for active encounter and creative engagement with the issues and challenges of the world today. *

---

* Rev. Dr Samuel Kobia, "Listening to the Voice of God", Christian Conference of Asia, Chiang Mai, Thailand, 2005.

The world is overwhelmed by competing voices. Many people ask how can the ecumenical movement respond to the voice of God when our senses and our common sense are overwhelmed? How do we hear the small, desperate voices of the impoverished, the vulnerable, the dying? How do we hear the raging of the disempowered, the disinherited, the destroyed? How do we hear the faint voices of those suffering and dying from HIV and AIDS and other diseases, the battered and abused women and their children who are trafficked for the world sex trade? How do we hear the voices of the migrants and refugees, the political detainees and the tortured, the political movements for freedom and justice for themselves and the plundered earth?

Whose are these overwhelming dominant voices that drown out the cries for a life of dignity, for the integrity of all creation, for the right to be different and included? There are many of course.

One set are the opinion makers, the forces that mould and manipulate all realities into commodities. The market and the media for, in today's globalized world, the one is the servant and master of the other. People, land, knowledge, work, politics, faith, religion are all measured according to their monetary value, while little or no value is attached to equality, compassion, dignity, rights, integrity which have no secure place in this market-driven world. These are the voices that tell us constantly that the ultimate purpose in life lies in our ability to earn wealth and to consume no matter what negative impact it may have on us, on others and on the environment.

Secondly, there are the voices that dominate our structures, our institutions and our relationships. These voices stifle and silence desperate cries for dignity, equality and justice – voices of fundamentalism and extremism in the resurgent religious right which domineer and spread fear and suspicion among people and communities. Minorities – whether religious, ethnic or linguistic – are increasingly violated and excluded. People are made to believe that in this world some, belonging to powerful nations, are more important than others and that injustice and inequality are legitimized in the name of God.

Thirdly, the voices that silence dissent through fear and brute power like the war on terror and the drive to economic globalization. These, and their allies, have already established a political culture that deals with dissent and difference ruthlessly to safeguard the interests of hegemonic powers. They tell us through their control of information and through their illegal and tortuous actions that the only way to resolve conflicts is through the exercise of violent power.

How then, do we hear the voice of God when the cries of his people are muted by those who want the powerful alone to define the shape of the present and the future?

We believe God listens and God speaks to the world and his communication with the world is endless. Moses hears the cries of the slaves in Egypt. Isaiah prophesies of the new Jerusalem where there will be no weeping and distress. Jesus responds to the excluded and the disempowered and Paul reminds us of the groaning of all creation for liberation. God listens to the cries for a reformed and transformed world, for a new order, for *oikoumene* and promises grace.

Therefore, should we not view the ecumenical vocation as a vocation for life and transformation, and a promise of grace? Surely and certainly, in a world overwhelmed by the dominant voices that silence the cries of people for justice and life, *oikoumene* needs to be a space where life is celebrated, where life is affirmed. Should we not then view the ecumenical vocation as a vocation for life and transformation? Our option to listen as God's people brings with it the need to search for responsible, bold and creative responses.

Listening to the voice of God in human cries for a more abundant life

If we are going to make bold and creative responses, then the multiplicity of ecumenical structures is a serious problem, but for the longer term we must address the *content* of ecumenism.

With the demographic shift from North to South now an irreversible reality, the influence of confessional theological emphases on ecumenism has been reduced. It has also become clear that doctrine is not the only issue that keeps Christians apart in many, especially multi-religious, contexts. The reality of a divided church is also a reflection of a divided world. War and violence, wealth and poverty, ethnic and tribal identities etc. have had their influence on the way churches understand themselves and relate to each other.

However, the ecumenical movement in Asia has pioneered something called Christian unity in action or the ecumenism of action around issues directly affecting peoples. These transcend the boundaries of tradition and denomination to listen to the voice of God in suffering humanity's cry for life amid globalization and the war on terror. The Christian Council of Asia launched a People's Forum on Peace for Life in 2003 at Seoul, Korea saying "… we are driven to reclaim the gift of life given to us by God… The urgency of the threat to life calls us all to a creative, concerted and organized response to rediscover peace. We challenge the churches, religious bodies and our partners to join us in furthering an ecumenical, interfaith and multi-religious coalition of people's movements and other groups."

This is part of a significant trend towards local, informal, trans-denominational ecumenical coalitions – the name dates back to Canada in the mid-1970s – around issues that concern people in specific geo-political contexts. They are not structured into institutional ecumenism nor are they concerned with theological differences. A certain degree of defiance to structures of authority and bureaucracy within ecumenism and historical churches is often noted. But they have their own rationale and dynamics. They are also a positive trend that signifies the experimental and experiential dimension of ecumenism.

Since the demographic shift in the 21st century, there is a new and distinctive urge to discover afresh the meaning of being church in different contexts. Should we then continue to rely on the legacies of the past ecumenical era, based as they are around traditional western theologies. Many Asian ecumenical groupings and theologies have challenged the relevance of western theological premises for the global ecumenical movement, as have other regional ecumenical members. It seems there is a an urgent need to turn to the new theological explorations "from below" that are emerging in active critical engagement with the issues of people's lives in order that we conceive our ecumenical vocation in a new way – as a creative instrument in the service of the unity and diversity of humankind.

Progressive social movements which might be called alliances for life are not some romantic preoccupation. They are taking upon themselves the responsibility of speaking the truth to power. They are also coalitions of resistance to injustice, oppression and exclusion. The churches that hold a commitment to life must come into new partnerships and relate to people of other faiths and ideologies. We cannot afford to close our eyes to these realities and continue with the old, traditional notions of people of other faiths and of mission. We must look positively at religious pluralism and grope for ways by which we may become active partners with others. In a world where fear of change, and fear of others are the major sources of violence – a view unfortunately promoted by the religious right – we look forward to learning the art of negotiating partnerships for peace from the Asian churches and ecumenical movement – "a wider ecumenism" or an "ecumenism of religious traditions" (Wesley Ariarajah) that transcend and run parallel to Christian ecumenism.

Towards a spirituality of life

In the midst of the rapid changes caused by globalization, we can see definite world-wide evidence of a phenomenal yearning for a spiritual way of life, manifested through spontaneous expressions of belief that challenge the churches' formality, structures and prerogatives. Doctrinal and theological considerations do not set the agenda. These outbursts of spirituality are evident in all regions of the planet and are post-denominational expressions of being church in clear rejection of the structures of the historical churches. Youth, to a large extent from the urban middle classes in the developing world, claim they are looking for answers to the complex questions of a rapidly changing world. The answers they are seeking so earnestly are not those of the dominant voices. Many are crossing boundaries of tradition that a few years ago would have been unthinkable, forming new spiritual and moral networks. Others are highly sensitized socially and want to participate in politics, social and economic justice, environmental protection, movements for peace and against hegemonic powers. Fearless of the old ways, filled with energy and vitality, these young women and men articulate their own visions of the world.

If post-modernity is robbing us of our capacity to be human and leaving us indifferent to the needs of others, how can we even claim to be Christian or ecumenical? The ecumenism of the 20th century arose from youth and student movements, from Faith and Order, Life and Work, but today it is no longer sustainable on these theological and organizational premises. Ecumenism needs new focus and new instruments to make present the unity and the diversity of God's people in spite of, and amidst, a world that changes constantly. And we must do this in a way that relates organically to the contemporary yearning for experiential dimensions of faith, especially among younger women and men. We must also ensure that it comes to be understood in terms and acts consistent with the spirituality of life experienced among the poor and their movements of resistance to overcome the shackles of poverty, violence and oppression. Otherwise, the spiritual yearnings of young adults will not result in the necessary changes in the lives of the poverty-stricken South, but serve only the emotional and materialistic needs of the middle classes.

Churches of all stripes need to dedicate, with great seriousness, all their energies to ecumenical formation in order to re-energize the ecumenical movement by creating adequate space at all levels. This began at Porto Alegre with more than 300 youth. Our next challenge is to change the structures that prevent youth from playing their rightful role, as they did long ago at Uppsala, Sweden, in the decision-making processes of the ecumenical movement.

As I returned from eight regional meetings and dozens of other events with people around the globe, and travels on every continent, I compiled a growing and changing list of significant implications for ecumenism in the 21st century which require urgent action if the movement is not to be stifled by institutionalism and structures:

- the decline of membership among churches in Western Europe and North America and their reduced abilities to contribute financially to the work of the ecumenical movement while increasing their ties to confessions and denominations;

- the reduced influence and status of these Northern churches in society, politics, governance, advocacy and common witness while turning inward for security to institutions and bureaucracies;

- the shift of Christianity's centre from the North to the South numerically, theologically and doctrinally and away from denominationalism, hierarchy and structure;

- the loss of modern ways of formation of youth, the decline of ecumenical youth movements, their energy and dynamism leaving a void from where ecumenical leaders for the future might come;

- the yearning for spirituality among people of all ages is compelling for the ecumenical movement but can it meet these needs when our structures have become too self-serving and top-heavy to cope with post-denominationalism?

- the tensions between ecumenism as a movement and its institutions is growing with the latter languishing while the former is thriving;

- the need to broaden ecumenical fellowship with evangelical, Pentecostal, post-denominational and Roman Catholic churches is critical but has yielded few results despite enormous time and resources dedicated to this activity; and

- the tension between a commitment to the ecumenical movement and confessional structures is unsustainable in their present configuration.

It is remarkable that the great world religions have survived for so many centuries and we may well wonder why as we watch secular empires wax and wane and ultimately disappear. The world's faiths embody truths that go beyond economics, politics and cultures and they remain salient even when all else changes.

We survive:

- not by our strength but how we respond to the weak;
- not by our wealth but how we respond to the poor;
- not by our power but how we are concerned for the powerless.

What history teaches is that what renders a religion invulnerable is the compassion it shows to the vulnerable.

As I travelled to new and old places, I became ever more aware of the global shifts that had occurred in recent years all across the religious world. It is both exciting and frightening to behold.

3. Mapping the *oikoumene*

Dawn is just breaking, but the congregation shows no sign of tiring. For more than eight hours – all through a torrid tropical night – they have sung, danced, moaned and prayed, led by a preacher many simply call Daddy. More than 300,000 have come out for this service of the Redeemed Christian Church of God at Lagos, the seething economic capital of Nigeria. Pastor Enoch Adejare Adeboye, a former mathematician, says it's just an average turnout for the fastest growing Christian movement on a continent that has become the demographic centre of Christianity, precisely located in West Africa in Nigeria, its spiritual home in the most populous nation of Africa.

Some theologians already say this is the African Century for Christianity. It is passionate, powerful and comes with a variety of names like Pentecostal, Afro-evangelical, charismatic, Christian renewal, evangelical and, more negatively, "Prosperity Gospel" which enriches pastors like Adeboye, who say that God has no problem with material wealth in a country where more than 70 percent of the 135 million people live on less than a dollar a day, despite massive oil reserves. Nigeria is regularly ranked among the 10 most corrupt countries in the world by Transparency International.

But, for millions, even billions, of believers around the world, these new movements of Christianity represent as sharp a break with traditional Christianity, as epochal as was the Reformation of the 16th century. Around the globe, Christianity is growing and mutating in ways that the churches in the West – especially North America and Western Europe – are only beginning to sense, let alone understand. From the Vatican to Geneva to London, the mainstream denominations too often view these new churches with fear and loathing because they are reshaping Christianity faster and more deeply than hierarchies and bureaucracies can cope with. Tumultuous conflicts within Christianity's 2.2 billion members will leave a mark deeper than Islam's in this third millennium.

Critics allege that these movements are too often based on shaky, thin and even cynical theology, exploiting the poor masses with "pie-in-the-sky till we die, bye and bye" promises. If you want to see where Christianity is heading come to Africa and look at Nigeria, or Kenya or Uganda, or go to the *barrios* of Latin America and across the teeming cities of Asia. It is impossible to miss.

Banners for revivals, healings, blessings, entertainment dot nearly every street in the religious hothouse that is Lagos (population: est. 25 million). One reads: "Nigeria is the nation which will achieve the kingdom of God that Israel lost in Matthew 21:41-44." ("...Therefore, I tell you, the kingdom of God will be taken away from you, and given to a nation that yields the proper fruit.")

Nigeria has hundreds, perhaps thousands, of these new churches, overshadowing Roman Catholics, Anglicans and other mainstream churches which came with the colonizers from Britain. Statistics are hard to verify in Nigeria but at least 63 million are Christians with almost as many Muslims. The new churches outnumber the religious mainlines by two-to-one.

The Redeemed Church growth dates from 1981 when Adeboye took over as "general overseer" (GO) and immediately claimed a role for global expansion. By the turn of the 21st century, he was claiming 5 million members in Nigeria and more than 250,000 abroad. "Daddy GO", as he is widely known in glitzy, noisy Nigeria, told the Associated Press (AP) in 2006 that his goal is 50 million members around the world, many of them in super-religious United States. Already he has held a rally in New York's Madison Square Garden which drew 7,000 for an annual conference. There is a city-in-progress called Redemption Camp. Redeemer's University has opened with 475 students and plans call for expansion in phases over 10 years. Dove Television is a satellite channel run from Dallas, Texas; Dove Link is a wireless Internet provider and there are Dove billboards, Dove music, a "Christian MTV" and two short-wave radio channels.

Daddy GO is pleased. "Our goals would require a lot of media preaching because there are quite a few nations of the world today where you just can't walk in and say 'I'm a pastor'," Adeboye told AP. "But you can't stop the message coming through the air. You've seen what they call military tactics: after you have done bombing from the air, then you can send in the ground troops." The tall, eloquent preacher radiates confidence, predicting that within 10 years the Redeemed Christian Church of God will be in every nation of the world. "And then in every town of the nations, and then in every village of the nations, and then in every home of the nations."

Adeboye doesn't discuss church finances in public but he made it clear during the nine-hour worship near Lagos that people, many of them poor, must give in order to receive. "It is clear from the word of God that you don't get out of poverty by praying. You don't get out of poverty by fasting. There's only one way of getting out of poverty. It's by sowing."

This plays into the hands of critics from the mainline churches. They say churches like the Redeemed raise false hopes and are so obsessed with world-wide expansion that they impose few standards on who starts churches or how they are run. "The pastors can basically do whatever they want with the money," said Samuel Bayo Arowolaju, a Nigerian-born expert on African churches, now living and teaching in Chicago. "The pastors of these churches become superheroes or mini-gods."

The mass media is filled today with stories about the influence of a resurgent and often angry Islam. It tends to ignore the variety and vitality, the global reach and shifting centres of gravity, the incredibly wide variety of practice and values that Christianity presents across the South. It is Christianity that will leave the widest mark on the 21st century. The process will not necessarily be a peaceful one and only the most foolish would predict what the religious picture might look like in eight or 10 decades from now. But the 21st century will almost certainly be regarded as a century in which religion replaced ideology as the prime animating and destructive force in human affairs, guiding attitudes to political liberty and obligation, concepts of nationhood and, of course, conflicts and wars.

Commentators who do speak of the changes needed in the churches today generally do not have in mind the sweeping historical aftermath of the first Reformation – but they should. For example, the steps that western liberal Christians suggest to resolve some of the churches' urgent issues could create unease or even revolt in some places or prove incendiary in others. The problem with change or reform is that people disagree, sometimes violently, on the directions it should take. Look at the Roman Catholic Church, a worldwide institution that is almost in fissure between liberal reformers who regard the hierarchy as aloof and arrogant and the conservative, orthodox leadership coming from the South. The liberal view, based on individual choice says Catholicism should become more inclusive and tolerant, less judgmental and more willing to accept western secular attitudes towards sexuality and gender roles. In the view of liberals, much of the current crisis of the churches derives from archaic, if not primitive, doctrines, including mandatory celibacy among the clergy, intolerance of homosexuality and prohibition of women from the priesthood. In their view, anyone should be able to see that God, the creator and lord of the universe, is concerned about human sexuality.

However, if we look beyond the liberal North, there is another Christian global revolution, quite different from the one being called for in American and European suburbs. Worldwide, Christianity is moving towards super-naturalism and neo-orthodoxy, in many ways towards the ancient world view of the New Testament: a vision of Jesus as the embodiment of divine power, who overcomes the evil forces that inflict calamities and diseases, wars and poverty upon the human race. In the global South (the area we used to marginalize by calling it the Third World), there are huge and growing Christian populations. Computer models currently estimate that by 2025 there will be 700 million in Africa, 460 million in Asia, 635 million in Latin America, and 30 million in the Pacific; in contrast Europe will be about 530 million and North America 235 million – now as distinct a form of Christianity as are Protestant and Orthodox from Roman Catholicism.

The revolution, or second reformation, taking place in Africa, Asia and Latin America is far more sweeping than any current shifts in North American or Western European religion, whether Roman Catholic or Protestant. There are increasing tensions between liberal northern reformers and the surging southern religious revolution. Despite still projecting relatively large memberships in European and North American churches, the numbers are often nominal and vestigial compared with the dynamism, optimism and confidence of Latin American, Asian and African Christian movements and churches. We look at such churches as the Redeemed Church in Nigeria with academic amusement only at our own peril.

Although Western governments are still struggling to come to terms with the notion that Islam might provide a powerful and threatening supranational ideology, few seem to realize the potential political role of an ascendant Southern Christianity. Rising religious fervour, no matter how bizarre it may seem to the ordered North, is coinciding with declining autonomy of nation states within a new transnational order in which political, social and personal identities are defined chiefly by religious loyalties.

Christians face a shrinking population in the liberal West. During the last half of the 20th century, the critical centres of the Christian world have moved decisively to Africa, Asia and Latin America and the balance is unlikely to shift back.

The growth in Africa has been relentless. In 1910, Africa had just 10 million Christians in a continental population of about 110 million, about 10 percent. In the first decade of the third millennium it is about 360 million of about 784 million, closing up to 50 percent. Christian countries in Africa have, despite the pandemics of HIV and AIDS, tuberculosis and malaria, some of the most dramatic population growth rates in the world. According to Martin Marty's computer forecasts, by 2025 the population of the world's Christians is expected to be about 2.6 billion – making Christianity by far the world's largest faith – and 50 percent of these will be in Africa and Latin America and another 17 percent in Asia.

The population shift is even more striking in the specifically Roman Catholic world where Euro-Americans are already in the minority. Africa has leapt from 16 million in the 1950s to 120 million in 2000 and is expected to reach 228 million by 2025 (*World Christian Encyclopedia*). Three-quarters of all Catholics will be found in Africa, Asia and Latin America. The map of 21st century Catholicism represents an unmistakable legacy of the Reformation and Counter-Reformation and their global missionary ventures.

All the figures we have actually understate the Southern predominance within world Christianity because they fail to take into consideration Southern emigration to Europe and North America. Even as this migration continues, established white communities in Europe and North America are declining and their religious roots are moving further towards secularism, liberalism and away from traditional Christian roots.

The results are almost unbelievable: half of all London churchgoers are black, African or West Indian; indeed those historic old piles such as Westminster Abbey, St Martin's-in-the-Fields or the great Central Methodist Hall would be empty were it not for tourists during the week and Afro-Caribbeans on Sunday who are now reaching out to whites though members complain that their religion is seen as a "black thing" rather than a "God thing."

For the first time in history an African-born prelate occupies the *cathedra* of Yorkminster and is Primate of England and Archbishop of the Province of York – the whole northern half of England. The Most Reverend and Right Honourable Dr John Sentamu, born in Uganda, was enthroned in October 2005.

Of 18 million Roman Catholic baptisms recorded in 1998, eight million took place in Central and Latin America, three million in Africa and just under three million in Asia – three quarters of all baptisms worldwide in one year. The annual baptism rate in the Philippines is higher than the totals for Italy, France, Spain and Poland combined.

The issue may be decided by global demographics which have huge, almost unbearable, implications for theology, ecumenism, religious practice as well as global society, economics and politics.

As Professor Philip Jenkins, of Penn State University, noted, in "The Next Christendom", even as Christianity is diminishing in the developed West the faith is experiencing an explosive growth worldwide. The centre of gravity of the faith is now squarely in the Global South. And there are many liberal thinkers and academics who don't like what they see. The liberal American Catholic writer, James Carroll, has complained that "world Christianity has fallen increasingly under the sway of anti-intellectual fundamentalism."

The Anglican dilemma

This trend is acutely felt in Anglicanism, one of the world's largest Christian World Communions (CWCs), with some 73 million members across the globe. More than half of all Anglicans live in Africa, South America, and Asia, where the faith continues to grow even as it recedes in Britain and North America. There are more Anglicans in Kenya (roughly three million) than there are Episcopalians in the US (2.2 million), and Kenya isn't the largest Anglican church in Africa. Church membership in Uganda is nine million, and in Nigeria is nearing 20 million worshippers. While the Church of England remains the mother church, and the Archbishop of Canterbury is the spiritual leader of the world's Anglicans, the balance of power in church politics has shifted dramatically.

That is why the future of the 450-year-old communion may turn upon the reaction of a few key Global South church leaders to the ordination of an openly gay bishop in the distant and tiny Episcopalian Diocese of New Hampshire (Anglicans in the US are called Episcopalians). The theology of these men is a direct legacy of the Church Missionary Society (CMS), a nineteenth-century undertaking by the evangelical wing of the Church of England to "promote the knowledge of the Gospel among the heathen". The fervent men and women who carried the faith to the far corners of the empire left a lasting imprint on their missions, and the churches in those countries are today led mostly by men who are themselves assertively evangelical and orthodox. They regard with dismay the liberal, progressive turn of the Western church, its willingness to rethink the fundamentals of the faith, and its apparent doubt about the plain meaning of Scripture. "The Bible doesn't make as much sense to them as it used to, to their ancestors," Henry Luke Orombi, the Anglican Archbishop of Uganda, says. "The interpretation of the Bible is no longer what it was before. And that's why the church life in America and Britain is so anaemic and feeble."

Orombi and other leaders of the church in the Global South believe that the current controversy over homosexuality directly reflects the divergence within the church over scriptural authority. For them, the Bible, Old Testament and New, is unambiguous regarding homosexuality – it is a sin to be repented of, and to be condemned by the righteous. In the view of these orthodox leaders, the acceptance of homosexuality in the American, Canadian, English and some European churches requires a reading of Scripture so innovative as to render its plain language meaningless. Peter Akinola, the Anglican Primate of Nigeria, has been outspoken on the issue, declaring that the Western church has so assiduously accommodated trends in the secular culture that it has betrayed the faith. "What is written of God is for all time, for all people. But when you take what is convenient for you, and you hold on to that, and that which is not convenient for you, you throw it away – then there is a problem."

Akinola is the acknowledged leader of the Anglican Church in the Global South, and as such he is possibly the most powerful figure in Anglicanism. He is, of course, subject to the prejudices of his own culture, in which homosexuality is taboo. Akinola has been quoted as saying that he cannot fathom the sexual union of two men, and that "even in the world of animals, dogs, cows, lions, we don't hear of such things." There is also a practical aspect informing the views of churchmen like Orombi and Akinola, whose churches are in competition with Islam. In the Islamic areas of Nigeria, for example, homosexuality is punishable by death, and Anglicanism's countenancing of gays complicates their evangelical mission. "Instead of proclaiming the grace of God, you have to justify that which God says should not be done," Akinola says. "Instead of putting your energy into the work of mission, you're spending your time defending the indefensible. It makes things much more difficult."

To the Global South primates (leaders of the autonomous Anglican churches or provinces are usually called primates indicating they are the first among equals of their regional church), such acts as the consecration of ECUSA Bishop Gene Robinson in 2003 without the broad assent of the whole communion reflects an arrogant indifference to the consequences. "If you want to be very blunt about it," Orombi says, "it's a form of neo-colonialism." Bishops from the former British territories were routinely frustrated when they tried to be heard at the Communion's once-a-decade Lambeth Conference of Bishops which brings together all bishops in the world. In 1978, Akinola's predecessor Joseph Adetiloye stood at the microphone for 20 minutes, refusing to be seated until he was recognized by the chair. "In ten years, when African bishops come to the microphone at this conference, we will be so numerous and influential that you will have to recognize us," he said. "In 1998, we will have grown so much that our voice will determine the outcome of the Lambeth Conference." And, indeed, at the 1998 Conference conservatives, with the support of most Africans, pushed through a resolution declaring that homosexual practice is "incompatible with Scripture" and church teaching. The Africans had laid their marker.

Traditionalist American conservatives see men like Akinola and Orombi as their natural allies, and, of course, as invaluable leverage. Global South church leaders have been inclined to help the efforts to supplant the Episcopal Church (ECUSA) as the official Anglican body in the US. They have opened mission churches in the US, and have offered episcopal oversight to dissident orthodox churches wishing to leave ECUSA and the Anglican Church of Canada, while remaining within the Anglican Communion.

It is one way, Archbishop Henry Orombi says, of keeping faith with those long-ago Englishmen with muttonchop whiskers who brought the church to Africa. "A hundred or so years ago, the fire was in the Western world," Orombi says. "And many of their great people went over to the countries in the Southern Hemisphere, and reached out there, and planted seeds there. And then things changed in the Northern Hemisphere... It now looks like the Western world is tired and old. But, praise God, the Southern Hemisphere, which is a product of the missionary outreach, is young and vital and exuberant. So, in a way, I think that what God has done is he took seeds and he planted them in the Southern Hemisphere, and now they're going to come back, right to the Northern Hemisphere. It is happening. It is happening."

It was in this light that some of the American conservatives began to look to the Global South. "It is simple," Akinola says. "We believe we know the mind of the Lord. We believe we know what he's asking us to do in his holy word, and we simply respond to his command... It is the power of the word, and the Lord has blessed our efforts." It is hard not to notice the contrasting results. When Gene Robinson arrived at the seminary to begin studies for the priesthood in 1965, the Episcopal Church claimed 3.6 million baptized members; church membership has fallen by more than a third in the 41 years since. There are more worshippers in Akinola's Anglican Church of Nigeria on any given Sunday than there are filling the pews of all the Anglican churches of the West combined.

Some of the weary westerners observe, by way of a small caveat, that the churches of Akinola and Orombi are still relatively young in the faith, less than a century removed from the missionary stage, their zeal uncomplicated by nuance. But the so-called classical Christianity of the Global South is precisely what appeals to many North American conservatives.

But it is much more than a brotherly regard for Christian piety that draws the Americans to the churchmen of the Global South. The conservative dissidents in the US already had the beginnings of a plan for what they called "realignment." By December, 2003, the initial outlines of the plan were revealed in a letter to potential supporters. "Our ultimate goal is a realignment of Anglicanism on North American soil committed to biblical faith and values, and driven by Gospel mission," the letter said. The aim was to create a "replacement jurisdiction" in the United States, supplanting ECUSA. The next month, in January 2004, the Anglican Communion Network (ACN) came into being. This effort was receiving financial support from foundations associated with the family of right-wing Republican Richard Mellon Scaife and other conservative donors.

The Archbishop of Canterbury, Rowan Williams, responded. He called for a church inquiry into the crisis, and the resultant commission findings, called the Windsor Report, urged the US and Canada to express regret over their action and to refrain from further consecration of gay bishops and the marriage of gay and lesbian couples. ECUSA apologized for any unintended pain it had caused the Church, but not for the consecration of Robinson, and it declared a moratorium on the consecration of all bishops, gay or straight. Canada acted similarly but could not guarantee that gay weddings according to prayer book rites would not continue.

A meeting of the world's primates was convened in Northern Ireland in early 2005, and some of them refused to share communion with their Canadian and American brothers and sisters (both Canada and the US have, unlike the rest of the communion, women bishops). At that meeting, the primates asked the churches of the US and Canada to abstain from the Anglican Consultative Council – the church's most important deliberative body – until after the next Lambeth Conference, in 2008. Akinola and others called on Rowan Williams to withhold a Lambeth invitation from the two member churches "unless they truly repent".

The Global South primates, in short, did all that the American conservatives could have asked, and more. When several of the primates appeared at an ACM convention in Pittsburgh in November 2005, they were greeted like rock stars by the 2,500 attendees. Akinola betrayed a hint of impatience with the American conservatives when he said, in his sharp, clipped tones, "Many of you have one leg in

ECUSA and one leg in the network. With that, my friends, comes disaster. While that remains, you can't have our support. Because, you see, as we speak here, we have all broken communion with ECUSA. If you want Global South to partner with you, you must let us know exactly where you stand. Are you ECUSA? Or are you Network? Which one?" Akinola said he found it hypocritical for American dissidents to encourage action by the Global South so aggressively while remaining affiliated with the Episcopal Church.

The Third Church

The denominations that are triumphing across the Global South are not just Anglicans in Nigeria but also many descendants of the historic mission churches. But it is the burgeoning Pentecostal, evangelical, radical Protestant churches, indigenous sects, churches for profit and Roman Catholicism of an orthodox kind that are stalwartly traditional and even reactionary by the standards of the economically advanced North. The Catholic Church which is growing rapidly, especially in Africa and Asia, looks very much like a pre-Vatican II faith, being more orthodox in respect for the power of bishops and priests and with a preference for older forms of devotions. African Catholicism is comfortable with authority and spiritual charisma much more than with northern liberal notions of process, consultation and democracy.

Meanwhile, a full scale Reformation is taking place among Pentecostal Christians many of whose ideas, especially in once staunchly Catholic Latin America, are shared by Roman Catholics. Pentecostal believers reject tradition and hierarchy but they also rely on direct spiritual revelation to supplement or replace biblical authority. And it is Pentecostals who stand in the vanguard of the Third Church. Although it emerged as a movement only at the start of the 20th century, mainly in North America, Pentecostals are today at least 400 million strong and heavily concentrated in the Global South. Some, like Jenkins of Pennsylvania State University, predict that by 2040 some billion people will be part of the Pentecostal movement, by far outnumbering

Buddhists and holding rough numerical parity with the world's Hindus.

These booming churches are thoroughly committed to recreating their versions of an idealized early Christianity – sometimes called the restoration of "primitive" Christianity – preaching deep personal faith, communal orthodoxy, mysticism and Puritanism, all founded on obedience to spiritual authority. Pentecostals and their Protestant and Catholic counterparts preach messages that appear simplistic, visionary, charismatic and apocalyptic to northern liberals. Prophecy is an everyday reality and many independent denominations trace their foundation directly to a prophetic authority.

Healing is central to these founding prophets who were able then – and now their successors – to cast out demons that cause sickness and poverty. The Brazilian-based Universal Church of the Kingdom of God offers "strong prayer to destroy witchcraft, demon possession, bad luck, bad dreams, all spiritual problems", and promises that members will gain "prosperity and financial breakthrough". The Cherubim and Seraphim movement of West Africa claims "conscious knowledge of evil spirits which sow the seeds of discomfort, set afloat ill-luck, diseases, induce barrenness, sterility and the like."

Northern liberals associate such religious expressions with primitive, rural people with little education and assume that modernization and urbanization will cause them to fade away. But in the modern Global South, in sprawling megacities, the spread of supernatural churches is enormous. Even in the North, observers can see the growth of Pentecostal and charismatic storefronts in inner cities. Often the new churches win support from migrations of rural people to the cities which lack the resources to meet their needs. In these settings, religious communities provide health, education and welfare. For people moving to developed countries to do the menial work their hosts will no longer do, immigrants group together in these new churches for community, culture, language and support as well as their faith. They become an alternative social system.

Often the new churches gain massive support for the way in which they deal with the demons of poverty, violence, crime and disease which are constant in everyday life, not through political action or even social justice, but by interpreting the horrors of life in supernatural terms: casting out demons, healing mind and body and exorcizing evil spirits. These churches often struggle against witchcraft which is a primary social fear among the impoverished.

In the desperate public health situation in the cities of the South where overcrowding, bad sewage and water, inadequate diets and communicable diseases are rampant, there has been an explosion of healing movements and cures for HIV and AIDS and other epidemics or the resurgence of old diseases. Today new churches rise and fall by the success of their healing and elaborate rituals have grown up around it. The same interest in spiritual healing is found in what were once the mission churches – Anglican, Lutheran, Methodist, Presbyterian and Roman Catholic hospitals and clinics still offer scientific medicine but for most of the poor it is simply beyond their reach.

Philip Jenkins argues that disease, pollution, alcohol, drugs and the violence associated with vast criminal networks can account for the reason people might easily accept that they are under siege from demonic forces and that only divine intervention can save them. "Even radical liberation theologians use apocalyptic language," he says. The answer to where this language comes from is simple: the Bible. Christians in the Global South read the Bible very seriously and believe it implicitly. When Jesus confronts demonic powers, especially those causing sickness and madness, he says: "Go back and report what you hear and see. The blind receive sight, the lame walk, those who have leprosy are cured, the deaf hear, the dead are raised to life and the good news is preached to the poor." (Matthew 11:4-5). Liberal Biblical scholars in the North have non-literal explanations for these passages but that of course is not how such scenes are understood in the Third Church.

The cultural gulf that separates northern liberal and southern orthodox Christians will increase rather than decrease in the coming decades just as northern and southern Europe was divided after the first Reformation into the Protestant culture of the word, preaching, singing hymns and Bible reading and a southern Roman Catholicism of the senses such as statues, incense, candles, processions and rituals. Southerners in some ways are still catching up with old technologies and cling to older ideals of community and traditional authority although the Third Church is rapidly learning the advantages of spreading its message by radio, television, and the internet.

As the Third Church grows and its leaders impact society more and more, it is reasonable to ask whether Christianity might also provide a guiding political ideology for significant parts of the world. We can recall widely revered martyrs such as Archbishop Oscar Romero of El Salvador, and Archbishop Janani Luwum of Uganda who spoke boldly and paid with their lives as modern martyrs. Across the Global South many leaders like Archbishop Desmond Tutu of South Africa, Dom Helder Camara of Brazil and the South Korean leaders helped overthrow repressive dictatorships and in Kenya church leaders keep a stern eye on political and social life. As the supernatural churches grow will there not be a new wave of politicians and even states in which political life and religious belief are inextricably bound together, much as Islam has always been? Zambia is a constitutionally Christian state and many others have talked of the notion in other parts of Africa. The liberal ideal of a clear separation of church and state, the democratic emphasis on human rights and tolerance and diversity, relationships between majorities and minorities and between rival churches and the use of laws to regulate private morality are all issues the Third Church will face.

With many new churches showing signs of authoritarianism and individualism, extremism among Christians also emerges, in movements which have grown up over the years. The terrifying Lord's Resistance Army in Uganda keeps parts of that country in terror, targeting children and women in one of the worst human disasters in Africa. The Lumpa Church in Zambia rejected all worldly regimes and a hundred thousand followers refused to pay taxes as they awaited the second coming of Christ, leading to confrontations with the government and open rebellion in the 1960s. The notorious mass suicides of the Jonestown sect in the remote jungles of Guyana in 1984 remind us how charismatic leadership can control people's minds and action.

Vast religious contests are already in progress in the 21st century. In Nigeria tensions and violence between burgeoning Christian churches and militant Islam have hampered the country's development and adversely affected interfaith efforts towards peace and reconciliation. Tensions between Muslims and Christians in the Philippines and Indonesia often have extremists from both sides at each other's throats. Hindu extremists persecute Christians in India. Demographic projections suggest these feuds could easily worsen.

The secular motif

In all these projections and scenarios, based on population growth, church vitality and the growing Third Church, the word "secular" comes to mind, especially for Western Europe and significant parts of the US and Canada. Europe will likely see a net loss of Christian numbers and move from first (in 2000 with roughly 540 million) to fourth (by 2025 with 532 million) among the continents. And North America, with one of the world's lowest population growths and a settled secular orientation in many of its parts, will likely experience little growth and remain the continent with the least Christians.

Martin Marty, the US church historian, uses the word "secular" to describe the spiritual, intellectual, moral and practical "envelopes" that surround the world of Christian ecumenism: "In contemporary times when an 'ism' got attached to the old term which meant 'profane or outside the sanctuary', secularism came to mean a systematic, often belligerent acting as if God did not exist or played no role in human affairs... ordinarily however 'secular' is more neutral, matter-of-factly employed for practical god-lessness in societies and cultures." (*A History of the Ecumenical Movement*, Vol. III, WCC, 2004). He argues that this led to a "differentiation" or chopping up of life into different sectors: religious from secular, this world from after-life, clergy from laity, fact from value, economics from politics, work place from home place and the like.

Denominations were part of a kind of "differentiated" Christianity and ecumenism in the last half of the second millennium was to minimize this "differentiation" and promote more unity and more core common styles of prayer, worship, mission and evangelism, social justice and education. But, in fact, the last four decades of the 20th century saw an increase, not a decrease, in denominations. Some statisticians say as many as five a week have been added to date and the number of Christian denominations now is well in excess of 25,000, of whom as many as 75 percent are Pentecostal and charismatic with at least 500 million members.

At a WCC Faith and Order Commission meeting in Malaysia in 2004, a prominent Pentecostal theologian from the US laid the issue straight on the line when he said the WCC must change drastically if it ever expects to relate in any meaningful way to Pentecostal Christians.

"Faith and Order has had absolutely no impact on Pentecostals around the world," said Cecil Robeck of the Assemblies of God. "It is easier to ignore 'them' than it is to take the time and effort to invite them, listen to them and give them the attention that is their due. But when the subject of these newer, growing, independent, evangelical, Pentecostal mega-churches is raised, North American and Western European churches tend to throw up their hands in frustration and despair."

Robeck warned that ignoring Pentecostal and other independent churches created a serious problem for the ecumenical movement because the Third Church will continue to grow at astonishing rates while, at the same time, many of the WCC member churches will continue to decline. "Where does that leave the WCC or your Faith and Order? You may not remember, but it is your churches that brought those new churches into existence. Like your own children, they think much differently from the way that many of you think."

Marty suggests this may almost render the term "denominationalism" obsolete. Many churches define themselves as para-churches or post-denominational churches with no real affiliations with other groups of Christians. This does not include the European and North American craze for spirituality with a wide variety of options in reaction to such things as secularism, materialism, globalization. Whatever it is, and from whatever culture or tradition, spirituality also is an alternative to organized religion and the institutionalized church.

One serious outgrowth of this "spirituality" or post-denominationalism or Third Church is the implications it has for the search for dialogue, and ecumenism. If these spiritual searchers disdain all existing and even new institutions, they will have little interest in dialogue and discussion between Orthodoxy and Evangelicalism, Roman Catholicism and Lutheranism or Christian-Buddhist dialogue.

Perhaps the most remarkable and troubling aspect of this Third Church growth with all its ramifications, is not the potential for conflict or the continued decline of traditional denominationalism or the challenges it presents to the ecumenical movement, but that these trends are so little recognized by even well-informed and well-connected Northern observers. What, after all, do most European and North American observers know about the huge growth, diversity, militancy and distribution of Christians worldwide? From my own observations after visits to every region of the planet, I suspect that most see Christianity much as it was when the WCC started in 1948 – a predominantly European and North American faith with a great many missions and missionaries overseas still trying to convert the heathen.

The wired and wireless world through the mass media has concentrated since the 9/11 attack on the US and the subsequent "war on terror" on an extremist view of Islam, but in doing so has created the impression that Islam, not Christianity, is the rising faith of Asia and Africa, the authentic or default religion of the world's poverty-stricken masses. But, as I think we have seen, Christianity is not only surviving in the Global South, it is going through a radical revival, a return to its scriptural roots and it is revolutionary in nature, just as was the early church.

In late August of 2004, I spoke to a group of Roman Catholic theologians which was meeting at Geneva. I quoted from Visser 't Hooft who said to Europeans that: "for ecumenical theology to flourish, it must be de-westernized." It was a prophetic note as I told my Roman Catholic friends: "Is it not high time to leave behind the destructive pride of the dominant global culture that has its origins in the colonizing drive to conquer and subdue the world?" I suggested that European theologians could learn from my African culture "where we believe that the world is a living shrine because human life directly depends upon and lives from the vital forces that come from the earth. As a result, the ushering in of a New World is organically related with the struggles to change the very world in which we live."

The problem is, as we examine and analyze the religious map of the world, by any reasonable assessment of numbers, the most significant transformation of Christianity in the world today is not in the liberal North, it is the third reformation coming from the Global South. And it's very likely that long before we are half way through the third millennium neither component of global Christianity (North and South) will recognize its counterpart as authentically Christian.

And as we see a bewildering, unstable, but vibrant and dynamic church in the South, so too we turn in our travels to the political and economic world of violence and pain where people cry out for hope and healing.

4. A world crying in great anguish

The New Testament records three major temptations of Christ. In the second (Luke: 4) the devil takes Jesus up to a high place and, after showing him "in an instant all the kingdoms of the world" says to him: "to you I will give their glory and all this authority; for it has been given over to me." (A view of today's world all too accurate for comfort!). The devil makes his proposal: "If you, then will worship me, it will all be yours."

What is the temptation then if not the ancient but timeless and also modern one of seeking status through power? The sin of Adam and Eve had nothing to do with sex, but everything to do with power. Adam and Eve took the apple at the foot of the tree of knowledge because they wanted power; they wanted to know more, to have more, to be more. "You will be like God," (Gen. 3:50) tempted the serpent, and they jumped at the chance, as to this day does the Adam and Eve in every one of us.

If the temptation was serious to Jesus, and almost irresistible to most of us, we can be sure that to seek power and status is a thoroughly irresistible temptation to a superpower and nascent superpowers. Speaking about nuclear weapons – and he could well have substituted all other weapons of mass destruction – the late Rajiv Ghandi told the UN in 1988:

"History is full of myths parading as iron laws of science: that the white race is superior to coloured races; that women are inferior to men; that colonization is a civilizing mission and that nations which possess nuclear weapons are responsible powers while those that do not, are not."

For years before and after the cold war ended and the Soviet Union collapsed, the world's lone superpower went on arming and rearming far beyond any defensive sufficiency or strategy of deterrence required. Over the years caused regime change in Iran (1953), Guatemala (1954), Iraq (2003), tried at massive human cost to impose itself on Southeast Asia, drove out the elected government of Nicaragua, ran – and still runs – a costly war against drugs and now terror. It propped up countless ruthless dictators like Marcos of the Philippines, the Shah of Iran, Hussein of Iraq and Mobutu of Zaire and was involved in the killing of

Lumumba of the Congo and forced two coups to oust Aristide of Haiti. And that's why many weak and authoritarian leaders today want to see to it that the US remains the sole superpower.

As always, the stated goal is lofty, this time it's the war against terrorism, to provide stability for a volatile world, some of which is resolutely resisting globalized neo-liberal economics. But if the world examines the basic interests of the superpower and its relations we have to conclude that, just as before, so now the primary concern is to preserve a status quo favourable to power politics, far more concerned with disorder than injustice. The invasions of Iraq and Afghanistan have done more to feed militant Islam than any preaching by radical imams. The prophet Amos (6:3) said to such nations: "You think to defer the day of misfortune, but you hasten the reign of violence."

More clearly than most, churches should know that no nation is served well by illusions of its own righteousness. All nations make decisions based on self-interest and then defend themselves on the basis of morality. Saint Augustine gave excellent advice when he said "never fight evil as if it were something that arose totally outside yourself." He was reflecting on St Paul's "all have sinned and fallen short" (Romans 3:23). It is tempting, of course, to believe that some have sinned – for example "the evil empire", or the "terrorist" Muslims, or "those who threaten our values" – or that most have sinned, but not us.

We are now living in what was supposed to be the morning of a new age. Unlike the bipolar world of yesterday's 20th century, the future we hoped and believed would be multi-polar, thriving on diversity. We did not need or want a single superpower, the innocent among us thought. We could turn our minds to fighting poverty, disease, injustice, corruption, and inequality. Innocence, in the sullied stream of human life, is beguiling but holiness is our only real alternative to a globalized economy, [un-] free trade and the imposed stability that props it up.

Churches all over the world and people of all faiths have a God-given responsibility to see that non-violence becomes a strategy, not only for individuals and groups and our beloved peace churches, but one taught to governments. If the burgeoning arms industry is to be reined in and wars become less high-tech, then new methods of conflict-resolution must be found. We must learn and teach nations to listen to one another. We must replace the concept of national security with that of common security, an understanding that the security of countries cannot be imagined separately, for none is really secure until all are secure.

The technologies today of communications and mass media, including the internet, have made it all but impossible to hide genocides, mass murders, mass starvation, and pandemics. No longer can most of us say "I didn't know", whether the destruction takes place within borders like Rwanda and Darfur or across borders like Iraq and Afghanistan. But how long do we mock God by moral isolation instead of moral outrage? How many times do we wring our hands and mutter the incantation of "Never Again" as the genocides and massacres continue? The new era, already upon us, reminds us that God is not mocked: we have to be merciful when we live at each other's mercy; we have to learn to be meek or there will be no earth to inherit.

For the healing of the nations

Into this world that is reeling from violence, where the danger to all creation is immense, where billions live in hunger and poverty, where diseases never heard of 50 years ago run rampant and threats of new pandemics are rife, we offer unity and peace. In the same world, where military technology threatens us all, where wealth and growth cause global warming and climate change, where people die of overeating and many more die of hunger, where human beings become commodities while information is processed beyond human comprehension, we offer equality amidst difference.

Into this world, the ninth assembly of the World Council of Churches came to Latin America to pray for healing: "God, in your grace, transform the world." Was it possible? Could there be a vision of the third millennium that God

78

could heal and transform this tumultuous world. Who is there big enough to love the whole planet? Yet a vision was essential. "Where there is no vision, the people perish" (Proverbs 29:18).

> The world seems today like Michelangelo's power-fully poignant Last Judgement in which the man at the centre of the painting is being dragged down to hell by demons, one hand over one eye, and in the other, a look of dire recognition. He understood, but too late. It's a familiar story. Why do we never see the truth until it stares us in the face? Michelangelo was right: hell is truth seen too late. Many believe, even in the churches where we acknowledge and confess that God can trans-form and heal this world, that we may be too late. We are broken in all our relationships. No longer is it the survival of a single nation, or even a group of nations as it was when the WCC was formed out of the bro-kenness of the Holocaust and the second world war, it is the survival of the planet. The chief religious ques-tion cannot merely be "what must I do to be saved?" but rather "What must we all do together to save God's creation?" Do we have a saving vision?

The ecumenical movement does have a vision: that prophetic vision from long ago of human unity is now an urgent necessity; that vision which says we all belong together, all 6.5 billion (and growing every second) of us. That's the way we believe God made us and Christians believe that Christ died to keep it that way. Human unity is not something we are called on to create, it is something we are called upon to recognize and make manifest. Disunity is a sin in all faiths and unity celebrates diversity. This is what people at Porto Alegre said they were yearning for, what the WCC is yearning for, what the ecumenical movement is yearning for, what Christians are yearning for and Muslims, Jews, Hindus, Buddhists and all the living faiths. A new vision of an old vision for this third millennium.

In the midst of this real yearning, though, what do we find? At the assembly we heard members of the US Conference for the WCC bring the participants at Porto Alegre public words of solidarity and confession followed by pleas for forgiveness:

> ...We acknowledge that we are citizens of a nation that has done much in these years to endanger the human family and to abuse the creation. Following the terrorist attacks on 11 September, 2001 you sent us 'living letters' inviting us into a deeper solidarity with those who suffer daily from violence around the world. But our country responded by seeking to reclaim a privileged and secure place in the world, raining down terror on the truly vulnerable among our global neighbours. Our leaders turned a deaf ear to the voices of church leaders throughout our nation and the world, entering into imperial projects that seek to dominate and control for the sake of our own national interests. Nations have been demonized and God has been enlisted in national agendas that are nothing short of idolatrous. We lament with special anguish the war in Iraq, launched in deception and violating global norms of justice and human rights. We mourn all who have died or been injured in this war; we acknowledge with shame abuses carried out in our name; we confess that we have failed to raise a prophetic voice loud enough and persistent enough to deter our leaders from this path of pre-emptive war.
>
> The rivers and oceans, lakes, rainforests and wetlands that sustain us, even the air we breathe, continue to be violated, and global warming goes unchecked while we allow God's creation to veer toward destruction. Yet, our own country refuses to acknowledge its complicity and rejects multilateral agreements aimed at reversing disastrous trends. We consume without replenishing; we grasp finite resources as if they were private possessions; our uncontrolled appetites devour more and more of the earth's gifts. We confess that we have failed to raise a prophetic voice loud enough and persistent enough to call our nation to global responsibility for the creation, that we ourselves are complicit in a culture of consumption that diminishes the earth.
>
> The vast majority of the peoples of the earth live in crushing poverty. The starvation, the HIV and AIDS pandemic, the treatable diseases that go untreated indict us, revealing the grim features of global economic injustice we have too often failed to acknowledge or confront. Our nation enjoys enormous wealth, yet we cling to our possessions rather than share. We have failed to embody the covenant of life to which our God calls us;

Hurricane Katrina revealed to the world those left behind in our own nation by the rupture of our social contract. As a nation, we have refused to confront the racism that exists in our own communities and the racism that infects our policies around the world. We confess that we have failed to raise a prophetic voice loud enough and persistent enough to call our nation to seek just economic structures so that sharing by all will mean scarcity for none. In the face of the earth's poverty, our wealth condemns us.

We have come to this Assembly grateful for hospitality we don't deserve, for companionship we haven't earned, for an embrace we don't merit. In the hope that is promised in Christ and thankful for people of faith in our own country who have sustained our yearning for peace, we come to you seeking to be partners in the search for unity and justice. From a place seduced by the lure of empire, we come to you in penitence, eager for grace sufficient to transform spirits grown weary from the violence, degradation and poverty our nation has sown, grace sufficient to transform spirits grown heavy with guilt, grace sufficient to transform the world.

This heartfelt cry, this litany of failure to sound a prophetic voice and take persistent action can be replicated across the world where war, violence, environmental degradation, disease, economic injustice, poverty, racism and exclusion are a sadly familiar story – a story made worse by the compassion fatigue people feel after the endless and mindless, voyeuristic repetition of horror without understanding, in the various mediums of communication.

Challenges of the 21st century to the ecumenical movement

In the American plea for forgiveness are listed the core challenges the WCC has been aware of since the collapse of the Soviet Union and the imperial rule of one superpower. How does the ecumenical movement manifest and implement its vision of a "festival of life", a just and sustainable world community in this reality set out so painfully by American brothers and sisters? Where does religion fit into this world that includes Christian fundamentalists like the religious right in the US and Jewish and Islamic extremists who wish to rule and dominate the public sphere of governance? Interchurch and interfaith dialogue is crucial in this atmosphere and must be at the centre of the ecumenical agenda, an agenda that is all too slow to change and move away from the priorities it inherited from other times.

> The other part of the story about Michelangelo's masterpiece, *The Last Judgement*, where the figure has one hand over an eye, illustrates our basic unwillingness, or inability, to accept unpleasant truth as we shield ourselves from its wounding accuracy.
>
> If that is the case with individuals, how much truer is it for nations and institutions like those of the ecumenical movement, churches and other faiths. The Bible is full of these stories of people unwilling to hear the truth. Jeremiah describes prophets who tell people only what they want to hear as false because they said "peace, peace, when there is no peace" (Jer. 6:14). And Jesus said "Do not think that I have come to bring peace, but a sword" (Matt. 10:34). Of course Jesus could only have meant the sword of truth, the only sword that heals the wounds it inflicts.
>
> Is this the reason that we have such great difficulty in confronting the horrible truth about our world today? We must not only read the signs of the times but we must also find a clear, relevant and articulate prophetic voice for now and into the future.

For the healing of the nations

And yet, there is no question we live in a world longing for healing, for a life of dignity in just and sustainable communities – yearning for a clear sound from relevant, articulate and prophetic voices. And not only people, but the whole of Creation cries out for relief, consolation, healing. We are confronted with such a serious environmental crisis, and we have somehow isolated the human species from the rest of Creation as if nature could not collapse, but we arrogant humans act as if we are not part of the whole created world. If the natural order goes, the human species goes with it. We listen in pain to the groaning of creation as St Paul expressed it in Romans 8.

Each year the hurricane and typhoon seasons increase in ferocity and destruction, torrential floods on one hand and terrible droughts on the other – these are no longer seasonal disasters we cope with, they have become massive matters of life and death, especially for the world's poor whether they live in the affluent North or the poverty-stricken South. Small island states are most vulnerable to the consequences of global warming brought on by climate change. No matter how industry-supported scientists may differ with environmental scientists in an attempt to confuse people and their globalized governments that global warming is not yet completely proven, poor farmers and residents of the melting Arctic lands know that something is terribly wrong and it cannot be repaired and returned to its natural state. The "greenhouse" effect caused by over-consumption of fossil fuels, mostly for automobiles and industries in affluent northern societies and emerging societies such as China and India, create carbon dioxide emissions which are destroying species at the rate of three to five a day, causing enormous physical distress to people who must breathe the polluted air, and worst of all causing enormous damage to the environment and human life. Climate changes also create new forms of injustice. Creation is indeed groaning and there is no assurance that God, having given stewardship of the Creation to people, will intervene to change the growing catastrophe that the human species, in its greed and materialism has wreaked on all other species and systems of the natural order. It is not plants, birds, fishes, animals that are destroying Creation, it is human action in defiance of all that we know that continues burning natural gas, coal and oil, as if there were no consequences.

In Porto Alegre, we lived our theme "God, in your grace, transform the world". It became part of our lives, our prayers, it helped us get through the issues of the world that we were faced with almost daily. "Through the assembly, we could feel the prayer as our companion and as the days passed, a deep sense of yearning for change, for healing, for transformation was almost palpable. Robina Marie Winbush, an African-American Presbyterian woman who preached "For the Healing of the Nations", brought it home to many in the assembly's closing sermon. Taking her cue from Revelation 22:1-5, Winbush took participants through healing and transformation and reminded people that even though there were many death-dealing issues, Christians are to live as though the reign of God is here. The theme was both acknowledgement and confession that we believe God can heal and transform this tumultuous world." (Njoroge, 2006)

The words are meant to give us hope but we were choked with despair and failure as ecumenists when delegates and other participants went into the comfortable air-conditioned plenary session entitled "Overcoming Violence" on Saturday afternoon, 18 February. On the stage was a Ugandan, Olara Otunnu, a former UN undersecretary for the protection of children. He was dressed simply in a dark brown African shirt. Amid the hi-tech entertainment style of many presentations, with theatre, music, dance in tightly scripted presentations and video clips dropping out of the ceiling, Otunnu relied on nothing but his passion for "Saving God's children from the scourge of war".

His words were like those of an Old Testament prophet telling the truth we did not want to hear, words that were harsh and made people cringe. Many preferred the softer style of 21st century communication. Otunnu's first words set the stage:

"When adults wage war, children pay the highest price. They are the primary victims of armed conflict. They are both its targets and its instruments. Children are killed and maimed, made orphans, abducted, deprived of education and health, deeply scarred and traumatized. They are recruited and used as child soldiers, forced to give expression to the hatred of adults. Girls face additional risks, particularly rape, sexual violence and exploitation."

Otunnu stood tall and told the assembled church leaders in no uncertain terms that people and institutions, many of them "good Christians", should be named and shamed for grave abuses against children, whether they be presidents or wealthy warlords, or bishops or "chefs" and their names and organizations would go to the UN for publication until they changed their ways and complied with the rights of children. Focus was on six especially common and especially serious violations: killing or maiming; rape and sexual violence; recruitment or abduction of children for use as soldiers; attacks against schools and hospitals; and denial of humanitarian access to children.

He turned to his own country as a gross example where the northern region of Uganda was the "worst place in the world today to be a child".

"The situation in northern Uganda is far worse than Darfur, in terms of its duration, its magnitude, and its deep and long-term consequences for the society and culture being destroyed. It is a comprehensive genocide." As some in the plenary hall shuffled papers, yawned, murmured to neighbours, and a few left, Otunnu stopped them, saying simply "Witness…

- **Twenty years of war:** The humanitarian and human rights catastrophe has lasted for more than two decades;

- **Ten years of concentration camps:** A population of more than two million, of whom 80 percent are women and children, have been herded like animals into 200 concentration camps mainly in the Acoli area, in abominable conditions, defined by staggering levels of squalor, disease and death, humiliation and despair, appalling sanitation and hygiene, massive overcrowding and extreme malnutrition. A relief official at Gulu said "people are living like animals. They do not have the bare minimum."

- **Staggering death levels in the camps:** The infant mortality rates are the worst in the world today. A World Vision survey reported 1,000 children die each week. "We have reached the worst category an emergency can ever reach." The UN stated in November 2005 that mortality rates in northern Uganda were double those in Darfur. At Gulu again, the NGO Forum noted: "The camp population is not coping anymore, just slowly and gradually dying."

- **Non-existent health care:** There are no medicines, no clinics, no treatment, according to the Internal Displacement Monitoring Centre.

- **Malnutrition and stunted growth:** Chronic malnutrition is widespread with 41 percent of children under five severely stunted in their growth.

- **No education:** Two generations of children have been denied education as a matter of government policy, condemning them to a life of darkness and ignorance, deprived of all hope and opportunity. Imagine this in the land that produced Archbishop Janani Luwum, the martyred primate of the Anglican Church of Uganda, murdered by the dictator Idi Amin in 1978.

- **Children abducted and brutalized:** Over the 20 years, more than 20,000 unprotected children have been abducted and brutalized by the rebel group, the Lord's Resistance Army (LRA). Some 40,000 children, the so-called "night-commuters", trek several hours each evening to sleep in the streets of Gulu and Kitgumu towns to avoid being kidnapped and then walk back each morning. The LRA is headed by self-proclaimed Christian fundamentalist "mystic" Joseph Kony, whose brutal tactics in his war with the Ugandan Defence Forces aims to turn the country into a theocracy with the Ten Commandments as its constitution. He maintains savage discipline over his kidnapped and brainwashed army and the women and children throughout Acoli-land, and is a successful military commander who has held off the Ugandan army since 1989.

- **Suicide and despair:** In the face of the relentless cultural and personal humiliations and abuse, suicide has risen to an alarming level, especially among mothers who feel utter despair at their inability to provide for their children or save them from starvation and death from preventable diseases. In August 2005, for example, 13 mothers in one camp, Pabbo, committed suicide.

- **Rampant rape, sexual abuse and HIV and AIDS:** Documented reports of rape and sexual exploitation, especially by government soldiers, have become "entirely normal". Human Rights Watch says: "Women in a number of camps told how they had been raped by Ugandan soldiers and it is extremely difficult for the women to find any protection from sexual abuse. From an almost zero base, the rate of HIV among rural communities has reached staggering levels of 30-50 percent – this in a country which has received high praise for coping with a massive pandemic in other areas of the country. The Gulu hospital medical superintendent reported that in 2005 27 percent of children tested were HIV positive; 40 percent of pregnant women tested HIV positive; and among Internally Displaced Persons (IDPs) 37 percent were positive.

This, said Otunnu to his staggered audience, is the face of genocide.

"Church people are unable to cope: everything in Acoli is dying," a weary missionary priest said, "the extent of the suffering is so overwhelming according to international benchmarks this constitutes an emergency out of control."

Ugandan journalist Elias Biryaberama visited the Acoli region and wrote: "I encountered unique and heart-stopping suffering... shocking cruelty and death stalking a people by the minute, by the hour, by the day; for the last two decades. These children, these women have committed no crime to deserve this. They deserve an explanation and reassurance of change from their president [Yoweri Kagata Museveni]: they deserved it yesterday, they do today and will tomorrow."

"Ugandans south of the River Nile and their friends do not know that there is a genocide taking place in northern Uganda," wrote P.K. Mwanje, another Ugandan journalist.

Cardinal Emmanuel Wamala, Roman Catholic archbishop of Kampala, in his Easter message of 2005, stated: "There is a genocide in the north that will continue if the international community does not intervene to stop the war." And, in an anguished plea, Bishop MacLeord Baker Ochola II of Kitgumu diocese in the North said: "All these cries from the people of Uganda show very clearly that a slow, but sure genocide has been taking place in northern Uganda as the world looked on, as it did in the case of the Rwanda genocide."

As Otunnu ended, he raised his eyes from the lectern and staring directly at the leaders of the WCC's 348 member churches told them they had a moral, religious and political obligation to recognize, denounce and stop genocide, regardless of the ethnicity or the political affiliation of the population.

"We look to you as spiritual, religious leaders to provide that prophetic voice and leadership. We look to you to denounce the genocide in northern Uganda. We look to you to mount a campaign to end the genocide and to dismantle the concentration camps."

"I cannot help but wonder if we have learned any lessons from the earlier dark episodes of history: millions of Jews exterminated in Europe, hundreds of thousands massacred in the Rwanda genocide, children and women and men systematically massacred in the Balkans, now Darfur and northern Uganda. Each time we have said 'never again' but it happens again and again and only after the dark deed is done do we do anything."

"I beseech you in the name of Jesus Christ to take a stand on the genocide in northern Uganda."

It was quiet in the plenary hall when Otunnu sat down. Some applauded but for many others it was too stark, his words hit at consciences wooden with the war and violence that sweeps across our globe. Quickly the lights went up, the videos began, the dancers and singers took over the stage and some wondered if we would soon forget his disquieting speaking of the truth, this prophecy.

What could such an assembly do about such evil? What could the churches, the ecumenical movement, the WCC say that would "take a stand?" It is difficult. The assembly passed a resolution condemning the violence and called on others to take urgent action but the prophecy had come to us.

Our world is crying – as it has often done in the past – for an end to war and conflict. This perennial cry for healing is a constant reminder of the state of our life together on this planet. If there is anything that remains the same from generation to generation, from one end of the world to the other, it is that this world is the scene of injustice and war; coupled with this are the perpetual longings of people for peace and justice. Today, more than ever, we are acutely aware of the reign of war and injustice, because we live in an ever-shrinking global village. Thanks to advanced information technology we can see from one end of the village to the other. We read about our village, we hear about our village, we see our village on television and the Internet. With selectively chosen breaking news, we witness events as they are actually happening and what we see is exceedingly depressing, although we seldom see northern Uganda.

We are also becoming more aware of our interdependence: that which happens to one end of the village is likely to influence, for better or worse, the other end.

This state of war and injustice is paradoxical. It is both normal and abnormal because it has become so common in our lives, especially for those who experience it only as passive observers of horror. Yet in our hearts we refuse to accept it as the norm or we turn it off altogether in a hopeless denial. What can I do? In dealing with this reality of war and injustice we operate with different visions. We neither believe nor accept that it is God's will for so many people to suffer so much – the shanty town dwellers, asylum seekers, the hungry, the children, the wretched of the earth.

Down through the ages, as well as in the contemporary world, human beings have wished there could be a way of ending wars without triggering yet another conflict. There is a longing for an ingenious way of peacefully ending war once and for all. In 1934, at an ecumenical gathering, the revered German theologian, Dietrich Bonhoeffer was visualizing someone who would call for peace in such a way that the world would listen. He thought the church could be that instrument. After all, he reasoned, the church was united in one faith in Jesus Christ, whom Christians recognize as the peace of the world. Should not the church be able to speak out with one voice against war?

The globalized world has become nothing more than one big marketplace, a gigantic shopping mall as the neo-liberal economy takes over. The Western idea of an enterprising, prompt, well-educated, efficient, dexterous, healthy young person not bound by anything has been launched and relaunched. Questions about meaning, truth, integrity or moral commitment are silenced. And yet, in spite of all this, we see that for many, life has lost meaning and clear direction. There is a longing for healing, but it is often inarticulate and difficult to decipher. In the midst of plenty, people feel empty. The great philosophical and theological discourses of the past seem to have lost the capacity to provide healing.

Deep inside us there is a feeling, an awareness that things are seriously wrong and something is badly needed. We fathom, though vaguely, and often as only swift flashes of realization, the need for a radically different lifestyle, for a new system of values that overcomes the growth and consumer-oriented materialist values which subordinate being and relationships to having and using. We are, in strange contradiction with our own selves, witnesses to the failure of modern imagination. And, as we look upon the blood-stained map of today's world, there is much reason for despair. In spite of ourselves and our actual acts and deeds, and in spite of our politics and our economics, it is our hope and vision that there will be healing tomorrow. The feelings, the dreams, the hopes of healing are deeply rooted in us. Walter Brueggemann could not have put this vision more succinctly and strongly when he said, "we shall fund, feed, nurture, nourish a counter-imagination of the world." (Walter Brueggemann, *Texts Under Negotiation: Bible and Post-Modern Imagination*, London, SCM Press, 1993.)

There is a longing for healing. If nothing else, this brings us together from our different visions and religious traditions. We see it in the many interreligious initiatives concerned with world peace and with religions as peacemakers. Religions are solicited to foster peace as an alternative to the use of religion to fuel conflicts. Interreligious organizations have been created to foster cooperation for global good among people of the world's religions, seeking to promote the realization of each religious tradition's potential for peace-making, engaging religious communities in cooperation around issues of shared moral concerns.

The challenge today is to seek a unity that celebrates diversity, to unite the particular with the universal, to recognize the need for roots while insisting that the point of roots is to put forth branches. What is intolerable is for differences to become idolatrous. When absolutized, nationalism and ethnicity, race and gender are reactionary impulses. They become pseudo-religions, brittle and small, without the power to make people great. No human being's identity is exhausted by his or her gender, race, ethnic origin or national loyalty. Human beings are fully human only when they find the universal in the particular, when they recognize that all people have more in common than they have in conflict, and that it is precisely when what they have in conflict seems overriding that what they have in common needs most to be affirmed. Human rights are more important than a politics of identity, and religious people should be notorious boundary crossers.

It is undeniable that present national policies and national structures are not only incapable of solving worldwide problems, but in fact exacerbate them. Thus, the future is slipping away from us. To preserve the planet we need minimally and immediately to moderate national sovereignty and increase global loyalty.

How we put flesh to these truths is our calling. How can it be accomplished? What are some of the stories we need to hear?

5. Parables for a new millennium

One of the most effective ways of communicating that Jesus used during his ministry was that of telling stories – parables. He used ordinary every day events to explain great truths. He used language effectively, even bluntly without obfuscation and jargon. One of the most difficult tasks facing the ecumenical movement, dedicated as it is to transforming the world, is not so much identifying the problems we face but offering hope that God will, indeed, in his grace, transform the world. Following are four short stories which illustrate problems that face institutions like churches and the WCC and how our structures make it so difficult for us to change.

1. How churches ended a world of bondage

In 1787, twelve men met in a London print shop. Nine of them were Quakers and three were Anglicans. It may well have been the world's first distinct ecumenical coalition, and it set itself an impossible goal, one which just over two centuries ago makes the problems that Christianity faces today something like a Sunday School picnic. They were going to stop slavery in the biggest, richest empire on earth. It was akin to the WCC taking on today's forces of globalization single-handedly.

They did not know then that they would be the forerunners of today's civil society. This unknown group of Christians whose hatred of injustice and enormous skill in promoting human equality, a concept unknown in their age, led to the 20th century struggle for the Universal Declaration of Human Rights.

Their motivation was the gospel, their enemy, and the kingpin of their age's globalized economic system, slavery, forced labour. And they achieved their goal, at least on paper and until the modern day, in little more than one generation.

To understand how awesome a task they faced at their first meeting, picture the world of that day. It was a world in which the vast majority of people were in bondage. Very few people were free. Slavery was normal, freedom the exception. The Church of England and its main missionary society owned huge slave plantations in the West Indies. So did the Roman Catholic Church.

There had always been slavery. It was taken for granted even in Holy Scripture. The ancient Greeks had slaves, the Romans had millions of them, even the Aztecs and Incas, who themselves became slaves to the Spanish conquistadores, had slaves. Slaves were treated with unbearable cruelty, they were never paid, they died young, they were chained and bound most of the time. This was the world just two centuries ago and, for almost everyone, it was unthinkable that it would ever change. Three-quarters of the people alive in the world of 1787 were in bondage of one kind or another.

But the worst of this demonic history was achieved on the Atlantic slave routes when 80,000 chained and shackled Africans were loaded into slave ships each year and shipped under the foulest conditions to the New World, the West Indies, parts of the American colonies and Latin America. It was globalization at its very essence.

These 12 devout Christian men, dressed all in sombre black, who met in the print shop, set about attacking the 18th century slave traffic from the west coast of Africa across the Atlantic to bring men, women and children to labour until death.

American and British historians and all sorts of writers have glorified and fictionalized the Pilgrims, the white immigrants who fled Europe and Britain in order to worship God in their own way. They were a tiny minority of the people who crossed the Atlantic to the "freedom" of North America.

"From Senegal to Virginia, Sierra Leone to Charleston, the Niger Delta to Cuba, Angola to Brazil, and on dozens upon dozens of criss-crossing paths taken by thousands of sailing vessels, the Atlantic ocean was a conveyor belt to early death in the fields of an immense swath of plantations from Baltimore to Rio de Janeiro and beyond," writes Adam Hochschild in *Bury the Chains: Prophets and Rebels in the Fight to Free an Empire's Slaves* (Houghton Mifflin, New York, 2005).

The wealth of Britain today, its cities filled with Victorian cathedrals, churches, statuary, palaces, multi-national corporations, was all built on sugar and sugar meant the backs of slaves who tilled the plantations, treated as harshly as many of the modern genocides. Indeed, it was a genocide.

The anti-slavery movement had none of the tools of mobilization that churches and human rights groups consider essential today: no paid staff, no electronic devices whatsoever (telephones, computers, internet, e-mail, photocopiers), only horseback for travel, no offices; the twelve had the full weight against them of the British monarchy, most churches, Parliament and the House of Lords, the general public, the media and, above all, the might of British devotion to making money from its vast empire. There were none of the usual benefits for the abolitionists like salaries, pension plans, health benefits, paid leave and the usual perks. It was a calling, not a profession. On their side only passion and optimism: their cause was justice, their God would not be mocked, and their ability to organize is still used and copied today in all sorts of good causes and campaigns. Perhaps the passion and optimism have been lost to the slick and the speedy and the security, but the abolitionists' organizing skills are still relevant to an ecumenical movement seemingly mired in structures and in a world where equal rights for many men, women and children are still far distant.

The British abolitionists were shocked when they came to know about slavery and the slave trade but they were convinced that as Christians they could end these evils and drive them from the empire and indeed, from the face of the earth. They soon discovered that injustice does not vanish just because God is on the side of the righteous: their setbacks were numerous and they were often depressed and discouraged. None of the thousands of people mobilized to fight the slave owners and the class establishment of Britain ever made a penny and their eventual success meant a huge loss to the Imperial economy. Scholars estimate that abolishing the slave trade, and then slavery, cost Great Britain almost two percent of its total annual income over more than half a century, many times the percentage most developed countries give today in foreign aid.

Passion and optimism were one thing, but it was also the abolitionists' ability to face defeat and lose time and again, then regroup, mobilizing peoples' outrage, and go back to the struggle with great certainty that they were on the side of right and God was with them. This ability to stubbornly regroup in the face of defeat is something modern ecumenism as well as civil society must understand. Perseverance, passion and optimism are needed as badly as technical skills today. People got outraged and stayed outraged over someone else's rights and the rights of *people who were not white*. The abolitionists inundated Westminster with thousands upon tens of thousands of petitions even when it was clear that abolition would damage the British economy enormously.

The campaign lasted 50 sustained years. They made the connection – which is still so valid today in the struggle for social and economic and environmental justice – between the near and the far. The abolitionists made sure that everyone knew that the sugar they ate, the tea and coffee and rum they drank, the tobacco they smoked was theirs through the brutal suffering of Africans. Today we need to learn to ask: are the stylish shoes our kids wear made by a child in Indonesia; are the fruit and vegetables we eat picked by Latin American campesinos drenched in pesticides and insecticides; what Asian child labourer with tiny fingers put together our computers; or what women hand-stitched our elegant clothing in Haitian sweatshops?

We are not fighting globalization for the first time at the WCC, globalization was invented by the Atlantic slave trade and the goods it produced for a mighty and wealthy imperial power.

These abolitionists, so Hochschild recounts, also were in the vanguard of every important tool used by citizens' movements in democratic countries today. Think of the glory days of the WCC's Programme to Combat Racism (PCR). It used the same materials and tactics as the abolitionists, adapted to the times. It had passion, optimism and outrage.

"Think of what you find in your mailbox – or electronic mailbox – today: an invitation to join an environmental group. If you say yes, a bumper sticker for your car, or a logo for your window. A flyer asking you to boycott Guatemalan coffee. A poster to put up promoting the campaign. A plea that you write your politicians to vote for a certain pro-labour bill. A notice that a prominent human rights activist is signing her book about HIV and AIDS. A newsletter about the horrible situation in Darfur. A meeting where a Canadian general is speaking on the Rwanda genocide.

"Each of these tools and many more, including consumer boycotts, were used two-and-half centuries ago with great success, started by those 12 Christian men meeting at 2 George Yard in central London in 1787," writes Hochschild.

From their successful crusade much is to be learned today for the ecumenical movement which should never doubt, as Margaret Meade said, "that a small group of committed, thoughtful, passionate people can change the world. Indeed, it is the only thing that ever has."

Today, we might call such movements "alliances for life" in the spirit of the social movements of Porto Alegre's "Another World is Possible". These progressive social movements are not romantic preoccupations. They are coalitions (like the abolitionists) of resistance to injustice, oppression and exclusion.

"God, in your grace, transform the world."

2. At the hand of man

As this was being written, new Berlin Walls and fences were nearing completion in Israel to separate Palestinians and Jews and as a land grab for Israel. A wall and fence was being proposed on the US-Mexico border to exclude further illegal immigration from South to North and American legislators were considering returning some 15 million illegal immigrants living and working in the US to their (mostly) Latin American homes using the National Guard to enforce these draconian laws. Illegal immigrants were also (allegedly) running amok in Britain and Canada. Some African leaders were considering throwing open all borders on the continent, while Spanish and Moroccan governments built fences to keep other Africans from leaving the continent for Europe. Botswana was building another fence to keep desperate Zimbabweans in Zimbabwe and bodies of other Zimbabweans were being fished from the Limpopo River, having failed to swim to South Africa. In Holland a Somalia-born woman member of the Dutch parliament was losing her (supposedly) illegal citizenship and political career because she had lied (supposedly) many years earlier to leave her ungovernable, unsafe homeland.

There are more than 20 million refugees, internally displaced persons (IDPs) and stateless people in more than 150 countries in the world, according to the United Nations High Commissioner for Refugees (UNHCR). This does not include illegals living underground, nor those who statistically do not exist. Statistics are meaningless in some ways except as indicators but in 2005 there were more than 15,000 orphans or unaccompanied children seeking admission to 21 European countries, about a third of them from Afghanistan.

In the past 15 years nearly 200 million people have migrated outside their country of origin searching for a new life.

These figures of course do not include HIV and AIDS orphans in Africa and other parts of the world who are thought to total more than 15 million and are expected to reach nearly 18 million by 2010. About 12 million of these live in sub-Saharan Africa and most of the remainder live in Asia where there are a total of 87 million orphaned children – orphaned for all reasons – the largest number in the world. Statistics about orphans only include those children between 0 and 14 growing up without the love and care of parents.

Child-headed households, once a rarity in Africa, are increasingly common in countries like South Africa and Nigeria where there are many more than a million AIDS orphans and in Tanzania, Zimbabwe and Uganda where the number is almost a million.

Of course, many know that more than 25 million people have died of AIDS since 1981 all over the world, but far fewer of us know that of the 6.5 million people requiring life-saving anti-retroviral drugs (ARVs) in developing countries, only 1.3 million actually receive them (UNAIDS) while more than 6,000 young people (ages 15-24) are newly infected each day.

We could turn to wars and conflicts but statistics are very hard to verify: the conservative but usually accurate *Wall Street Journal* estimated that almost 37 million people were killed in the past century by wars of one kind or another – civil, cross-border, regional and world. That is more than the entire population of Australia today and the vast majority of those killed were women, children and other civilians, non-combatants, innocents.

During the 20th century and through into the 21st century there have been several genocides: the Armenian (1915-16, one million dead), the Jewish Holocaust (1939-45, six million dead), the Cambodian (1975-79, two million dead), the Rwanda genocide (1994, one million dead) and, although genocide experts may argue the fine points of law, there were also genocides in Kurdistan (1987-88, 182,000 dead), Bosnia (1992-95, 200,000 dead) and Sudan (South Sudan 1955-72 and 1983-2004, two million dead) and Darfur (2002-2006, 450,000 to date dead). After each genocide, the international community of which the ecumenical movement is a part wrung its hands, wept, passed resolutions and said "never again" and usually offered the lame excuse that no one knew it was a genocide or thought it was just a another civil war.

The vast majority of people killed in all these genocides were innocent civilians, especially women and children. Genocide, committed by governments against their own people, is a messy and complicated act of horror and both the UN and governments are extremely reluctant to name it. Thus, the debate that is ongoing in 2006 about whether the Armenian genocide, which occurred 90 years ago, and the Darfur genocide today can be properly called genocides. These abstract discussions can rage in bureaucratic and international legal circles but the fact remains that very few, including churches, did anything about them and the hundreds of smaller ethnic cleansings, racist actions, liberation struggles, civil wars and undeclared conflicts that have occurred in the past millennium.

And today, one of the largest massacres in history occurs in the eastern areas of the Democratic Republic of the Congo (DRC) where by mid-2006 at least 4.5 million civilians had been killed, many at the hands of militia factions supported by neighbouring states.

The fact that the vast majority of the victims of genocide are racial, ethnic, political or religious minorities needs to be emphasized by Christian churches and other faith groups because genocides have one thing in common, they are premised on the politics of exclusion and power.

If the above litany of horror is not enough to seize our consciences, we could continue with the Creation, the environment in which God placed all species, which the hand of man – and no other species – is destroying at a mad rate in what some environmentalists are calling the ultimate genocide.

Sometime in this century, the day will arrive when the negative human influence on the environment, particularly the climate, will overwhelm all natural factors. Since the start of the third millennium, the world has seen the most powerful El Niño ever recorded, the most destructive hurricane in 200 years, the hottest European summer on record (which killed 26,000 people in two months) and the first South Atlantic hurricane ever recorded.

With one out of five living things predicted to be made extinct on this planet due to the levels of greenhouse gases, the world is at the tipping point environmentally. Burning fossil fuels at the rate of 1,000 barrels per second, the human population is solely responsible through greed, irresponsibility and an economic system called globalization which is based on material wealth for a few and desperate poverty for billions.

However, it is possible for us to reverse this brief description of the challenges that face us in the ecumenical movement. Included in the growing list of course are:

- a growing global epidemic of cancer caused, many experts say, by a toxic environment due to the increasing use of chemicals in industry, pharmaceuticals and defence manufacture. Cancer is now the leading cause of premature death in the developed world. New diseases and pandemics such as the predicted avian flu threaten the lives of millions.

- the internet has enormous positive uses in the quick dissemination of masses of information, but its unregulated nature leaves many vulnerable people open to exploitation and manipulation. Billions have no access to this technology, widening the huge gap between the global North and South leaving the developing world further behind and unable to catch up.

- poverty is the state of life for the majority of the world's people and nations:
  - half the world – nearly three billion people – live on less than two dollars a day;
  - the GDP (Gross Domestic Product) of the 48 poorest nations (a quarter of the world's countries) is less than the combined wealth of the world's three richest people;
  - nearly a billion people in the first decade of the 21st century cannot read a book or sign their own names;
  - less than one percent of what the world spent on armaments was needed to put every child into school at the beginning of the third millennium, but it didn't happen; and
  - one billion children (one of two) live in poverty, 640 million live without adequate shelter, 400 million have no adequate access to clean water, and 270 million have no health care.

For these and many other reasons, the ecumenical movement prays "God, in your grace, transform the world." But we are God's agents of change. We cannot, perhaps, imagine a world free of conflict, for there are always dissensions which some are prepared to fight over. But, we can imagine a world free of violent conflict, an end to the HIV and AIDS pandemic, an end to genocide and ethnic violence, a world free of grotesque poverty, a world whose environment is clean enough to survive, a world free of sexual violence.

If this seems hopelessly utopian that may simply reflect how far we have slipped behind in an agenda we should have kept had we been serious about saving the planet and its oikoumene. Churches and other faiths must work together now to develop a single ethic of global responsibility.

"God, in your grace, transform the world."

3. Using bad language

Telling a true story usually puts the writer at odds with some sort of conventional wisdom in any institution, let us say traditional institutionalized churches. Some people call them "sacred cows." Cedric Mayson, a Methodist pastor and writer from South Africa with close ties to the African National Congress (ANC) once wrote a book entitled *Jesus, and the Sacred Cows: the Message of Jesus for the World Today* (Marshall Pickering, London, 1987). It came out during the darkest days of apartheid South Africa and punctured many of our institutional sacred cows that have nothing whatsoever to do with belief or faith. These cows usually have much more to do with office politics or bureaucratic inertia. Governments and the UN, even corporations, are like that too, they begin to believe their own propaganda and actually read their own press releases.

One of the sacred cows is the language we use. Our special language at WCC is "ecuspeak". More recently, an ecuspeak adapted to the dead languages fitted out for television or video and better business communication. Our newfound language – the art, really of talking or writing but saying nothing – has had to be swept clean of improvized literary devices, downsized into data power points, reduced to an industrial waste product.

Numerous graduates of business school and communications theory institutes (including many seminaries), and other management bystanders, most of whom applaud as if discovering a new wonder of the world, have duly noted this achievement. Never has so much information been instantly at hand, not only on a cell phone or blackberry and the internet but also in elaborate posters and logos on store walls and sporting stadiums and church halls. The promoters of the brave new world like to say that the "key outposts" and "innovative delivery strategies" broaden our horizons and brighten out lives with better-looking celebrities, more books available on Amazon.com, quicker access to "valued customers and clients" and a finer class of politician and bureaucrat capable of distinguishing between "core" and "non-core" promises.

Maybe some people who haven't had the advantages of church business and communications training in two-week workshops miss "key performance indicators" or misinterpret the "risk assessments" but how can anyone's life be enriched – whether it be a Swedish citizen, an American Republican, a Kenyan teacher or an Iraqi national introduced to the joys of Operation Enduring Freedom – if the language they use is disposable? How do people ministering to Christians in most of the Global South "derive synergies" from well-placed "knowledge entities"? The problem is that unfortunately we have adopted the use of a language emptied of meaning which is meant to serve corporations and governments and many NGOs and church headquarters. However, the words don't "empower" or "enhance" people who would find in their freedoms of thought and expression a voice, and therefore a life, that they can recognize and comprehend as their own. What is meant by truth doesn't emerge from a synonym for liberty, doesn't emerge from a collection of facts or an assimilation of doctrine, nor does it come from a declaration of war or even the blessing of a church. Truth is synonymous with the courage that individuals and groups of persons derive from finding a story that settles the wilderness of their experience with the fence posts of a beginning, a middle and an end.

Which is why we should be looking for people of diversity, who are willing to think out loud, to experiment with new narrative and story, take a chance with an argument or a line of inquiry that in other institutions might be snuffed out as ill-advised, untidy, overly complex or whatever other exclusions there are in the conventional wisdom of institutional life and work. In the kind of transformation we are looking for, absolute agreement doesn't matter as much as the person thinking it and articulating it. For example, the mission statement "What We Stand For: Our Core Beliefs and Values" could easily be written for the WCC except that those words – using the vaunted "industrial waste of throw-away language" taught as communications theory – are the preface for the mission statement of the Central Intelligence Agency (CIA) which in the same dead language further states: "Objectivity is the substance of intelligence, a deep commitment to the customer in its forms and timing". Does anyone know what that means? And does it not mean anything goes? Old editors in the WCC and elsewhere had a deep and abiding mission to eliminate this kind of gobbledegook. Once it might have been funny, now it is dangerous.

All too often churches and the ecumenical movement and the WCC publish critical facts and analysis, but they are usually far too careful in tone, trying to publish notes for a brighter tomorrow, a more hopeful optimistic world and – that, of course, is much of what we are about, hope – blueprints for a better tomorrow. That's all well and good but we need also to be rooted in reality, in knowledge and not be too naïve. Part of our job is to point out flaws in the system, to draw attention to government venality and injustices towards all. Only politicians (including church politicians) have ready answers to all the questions of the day and carelessly scatter their "solutions" to the four winds. We should offer helpful suggestions and tools for forward-looking change but we should do it as Jesus and the prophets did; by telling the clear, unvarnished, un-nuanced truth in words and language that are inclusive of all, not simply those who have access to "power-point literature". The impetus towards social, political and ecclesiastical change stems from the use of language that induces a change of heart, as our great speakers like Philip Potter, who prefaced this book, well knew.

In 1946, the well-known and much-maligned George Orwell made the point in an essay "Politics and the English language." The slovenly use of words, he said, "makes it easier for us to have foolish thoughts... If one gets rid of these habits one can think more clearly, and to think clearly is a necessary first step toward political regeneration." Or, in WCC's theme prayer language, "a necessary step towards being God's agents in transforming the world."

Or, more simply, how do we expect to find a brighter future for all Creation unless we can imagine it as something other than a Dubai resort hotel (see parable 4) or build a better tomorrow unless we have the words with which to construct it?

The decay of public language in the mouths of officials (politicians, publicists, marketing directors, communications experts) has often been remarked upon over the last decades, including our own beloved ecuspeak with its barrage of acronyms and jargon. People who truly communicate well do not learn that art by taking courses from WACC (World Association of Christian Communication). One of the best, Lewis Lapham, a noted practitioner of clear language and recently retired editor of *Harper's* magazine, says that today's public communication is "a ceaseless burbling of lies, no matter how 'context sensitive' or 'prioritized' and cannot long sustain either the hope of individual liberty or the practice of democratic government."

Lapham continues: "The collateral damage to all this audible silence is the increasingly hostile attitude towards the use of language that fails to conform to the standard of cable television. As steadily larger numbers of people, both North and South, get their "infotainment" or corporate entertainment in tone, substance, sense and feel of the thing, the difference between beer commercials, docudramas and soap operas becomes indistinguishable and they become irritable if forced to think.

"Subordinate clauses are viewed with suspicion by these communicators, parentheses are regarded as elitist and therefore condescending, messages and press releases must be delivered deodorized and free of ambiguity which is disturbing and therefore wicked."

A fine book, *A Nation Gone Blind: America in an Age of Simplification and Deceit*, by Eric Larsen (2006) approaches its topic from the perspective of a college English teacher alarmed by the progress that the last two generations of students have made towards the notion of the classroom as entertainment. The young inheritors of the world's supreme military and economic power apparently [according to Larsen] take it as an insult if anybody invites them to think. Why should they? Thinking isn't advertized on television or the internet. This is the new globalized communications where everything good is easy, anything difficult is bad and the customer is always right.

"God, in your grace, transform the world."

4. Why the developing world keeps losing

On the main street of the global economy in a place where all the roads and diversions created by free trade, immigration, open borders, closed borders, mass tourism and the jetliner intersect, there stands a city-state that is being promoted as the commercial capital of the 21st century.

I've never been to Dubai, but I feel like I know the place because whenever I see the slick brochures of that city-state or watch the million-dollar adverts on television and the internet, I see a neat and disturbing projection of how the rich visualize the future. It is not at all like that portrayed in the related parable, "At the hand of man."

One day this year, I watched a documentary about Dubai and I was struck, as most people are, by the scale and ambition of the projects being planned there. Things like the three offshore Palm Islands that fan across the sea, each the size of Manhattan. There's also the Burj Dubai, said to be the world's tallest tower and the only "seven star" hotel on the planet. The hotel is shaped like a sail, topped off with a helipad. Dubai is the kind of place designed for the masters of the universe.

I had always thought Dubai was built on oil and natural gas until I found out it is only six percent of their economic picture. Dubai has replaced dirty fossil fuels with tourism and promoting itself as a business hub where "1.5 billion people are within two hours flying time."

Perhaps the most awe-inspiring thing is the airport to be finished by 2020, bigger than London's Heathrow, New

York's JFK, and Paris' Charles De Gaulle combined. And the jewel in this crown is the new jumbo Airbus 380 that will bring in up to 800 people per flight. Tourism, as people at the WCC well know, leaves a distinct ecological footprint on the planet and one cannot help but wonder if this city-state is really a departure from the hydrocarbon-propelled world or merely a refinement, the final destination?

It seems a huge and somewhat demonic irony of mass tourism that when parts of the world are building walls and fences and draconian immigration laws against Africa and Latin America and Asia to keep people out, others are being seduced with glittering incentives to travel. It is like the irony of free trade where the North can erect walls of subsidies and tariffs but refuses to allow the South to play on an even playing field.

Or the irony of countries which allow their citizens to travel abroad to receive cheap medical care in places like the US and India, thereby jumping the queue in their home country's public health service while gutting Africa of desperately needed health workers – doctors and nurses especially.

But the traffic patterns have been set for a long time, perhaps since colonialism and the slave trade: the developed world takes from the developing world, then puts up barriers to prevent completing the inevitable loops.

Now, if you think a bit about the macroeconomics of all this, you will eventually arrive in Dubai.

"God, in your grace, transform the world."

6. God, in your grace, transform the World Council of Churches

If you trap the moment before it is ripe
The tears of repentance you'll certainly wipe
But if once you let the ripe moment go
You'll never wipe off the tears of woe.

The ninth assembly of the WCC believed the moment was ripe for transformation and, as the poet and mystic, William Blake (1757-1827) warned, we must not let the ripe moment go, we must grasp it now without hesitation, without fear, without ambivalence. We must learn to think straight, to act straight and to talk straight as did the prophets and Jesus and the apostles.

The "ripe" moment at Porto Alegre left a clear framework for the WCC to continue and strengthen its role as "the privileged instrument" of the ecumenical movement in the search for visible Christian unity. The assembly, perhaps reflecting the deep yearning for healing, peace, justice and enduring hope among God's people, set four major areas of engagement for the future programmatic work of the Council:

- unity, spirituality and mission;
- ecumenical formation;
- global justice; and
- public voice and prophetic witness to the world.

The assembly wisely did not attempt to set out a packed agenda of issues, leaving the actual reconfiguration to the Executive and Central Committees to work out with the staff. Meeting midway through 2006, the Executive took these four areas, debated them and clearly set out how they cover the whole range of issues that Christianity – within and without the ecumenical movement – is struggling with, regardless of the traditional language sometimes used. Actually it reworded them slightly to make six programme areas of activity for the Council as guiding principles of all its work:

- WCC and the ecumenical movement in the 21st century;
- unity, mission and spirituality;
- public witness, confronting power, affirming peace;

- justice and diakonia;
- ecumenical and faith formation; and
- inter-religious dialogue and cooperation.

It is a call to action and engagement and prepares the ground for a more integrated and proactive style of work in keeping with the challenges of the 21st century.

The divine *all*

In his own inimitable style, the man some affectionately call "God's scamp", Archbishop Desmond Tutu, the anti-apartheid fighter from South Africa and long-time ecumenist and seeker of unity, impatient as always with ecclesiastical cant, told the participants at Porto Alegre that God has a dream: "He longs desperately for the time when *all* his children know they belong to one family. In this quest, the WCC is crucial, as God's instrument for engaging us to realize God's dream." Tutu speaks always as if God were right beside him, and he chatters away to God and God to him. It is profound and dynamic. "We don't take seriously enough that God is God of all. We are far too easily prone to excommunicate others because we can't stand the fact that God welcomes all. I'm glad God is God."

Inclusion must be the key word for the ecumenical movement. There can be no outsiders. Exclusion is sin. Or, as Tutu puts it: "I reckon the most revolutionary words Jesus uttered were those he spoke to Mary Magdalene in the garden, 'go and tell my brothers that I am ascending to my father and your father, to my God and your God'. He called these men, these abject cowards, his friends and apostles, one who had betrayed him, another who denied him not once but three times, and who had all abandoned him. He did not say 'those so and so's' but, breathtakingly, 'my brothers'."

The essence of Tutu's joyous plea for unity is not some impractical dream, it is reality and his impatience is with those who would use stagnating structures, or outworn institutions, or apartheid-like exclusions to make some people or groups or denominations or faiths into outsiders. "Jesus, it seems, was quite serious when he said that God was our father, that we belonged *all* to one family, because in this family *all*, not some, are insiders. None is an outsider. 'I, if I be lifted up, will draw all – black and white, yellow and brown and red, rich and poor, educated and not educated, beautiful and not so beautiful, Christian, Muslim, Buddhist, Hindu, atheist, women, men, gays, lesbians, and so-called straights, *all* belong, *all* are held in a divine embrace that will not let us go – *all*, for God has no enemies and, least of all my enemies are not God's enemies."

The ethic of the family has been used for centuries to symbolize the church, to describe the community of people. The family means from each according to their ability, to each according to their need. "How?" asks Tutu, "if we are a family can we spend such obscene amounts on budgets of death and destruction when we know that a small fraction of the money spent on these weapons of mass destruction would ensure that God's children everywhere, our sisters and brothers, would have enough food to eat, clean water to drink and would have acceptable and affordable health care, decent homes and a good education?

"We will not, we cannot win a war against terror as long as there are conditions of poverty and squalor, ignorance and disease that make some members of our community of *all* God's children desperate and excluded."

A united church is not an optional extra to Christianity. A united church is indispensable for the transformation of God's world, the vision of St John the Divine:

> *After that I looked and saw a vast throng, which no one could count, from all races and all tribes, nations and languages, standing before the throne and the lamb. They were robed in white and had palm branches in their hands and they shouted aloud: Victory to our God who sits on the throne and to the lamb! And all the angels who stood around the throne and worshipped God, crying Amen! Praise and glory and wisdom, thanksgiving and honour, power and might be to our God forever.*
> (Rev. 7:9-12)

Disentangling from the past

In 2008, the WCC is expected to celebrate its 60th anniversary (its diamond jubilee for those who follow such celebrations) at a time in history when, as we have seen in chapter three, Protestantism is in such a state of decline that some pundits are predicting it will no longer be one of the main pillars of the ecumenical movement. Protestants were the creative force and the backbone of the WCC and all the regional, national and international ecumenical bodies (e.g. the Student Christian Movement (SCM), the World Student Christian Federation (WSCF), the Young Men's and Women's Christian Associations (YM and YWCA) and Action by Churches Together (ACT)). They are still the primary donors to the WCC and the main confessional bodies.

But Protestants in Europe and North America have lost a lot of their clout with national governments, they are in financial trouble, many of them living on their legacies and investments, their membership aging and their once magnificent buildings which vibrated with Sunday worship are more like museums to another era. In North America, a shift to extreme right-wing conservative theology has followed the shift to extreme right-wing ideology for about half the Christians in the US. Influence, both in moral and political arenas is also in decline. Mainline church leaders no longer have easy – or even any – access to the beltways of power in Washington. Support, both financially and with personnel, and influence on governance policies are bound to be reduced making traditional church-state relations irrelevant while new churches unrelated to traditional Protestantism are regularly invited to the White House. The highly privileged position of mainline churches with governments is being replaced by non-WCC churches.

It is true that similar changes are under way in Roman Catholic churches in the North and also in Latin America. These same pundits who predict the near demise of Protestantism suggest that the three pillars of ecumenism in this century might well be Orthodox, Roman Catholic and a combination of Pentecostals and evangelicals.

One of the difficulties the WCC must face in its reconfiguration process is exactly where confessional bodies and denominationalism will fit with the "divine *all*" that Archbishop Tutu so eloquently espouses. What will it mean to the WCC in the process of reconfiguration laid out by the ninth assembly? Will it concentrate, as it has largely done for at least the last decade, on restructuring and reorganization mainly of the Geneva headquarters, or will it move to renew and recapture the spirit of an ecumenical movement?

Or, as one Latin American evangelical theologian, Dr J. Norberto Saracco of the Good News Evangelical Church of Argentina said at Porto Alegre, "the current way of doing ecumenism has gone as far as it can go. The ecumenical agenda must disentangle itself from the past and become open to the future. In Latin America, we are entering into a post-Pentecostal era, which will create better conditions for ecumenical dialogue". Referring to the text of his later speech to a plenary session on church unity, he said, "For evangelical churches, unity is not based on the recognition of a hierarchical authority, nor on dogmas, not on theological agreements, nor on alliances between institutions. We have to accept that that way of doing ecumenism has gone as far as it can."

And in a powerful address to the assembly, retiring Moderator of the Central Committee, Catholicos Aram I warned us that a church as divided as it is today, "cannot offer a credible witness in a broken and violent world and cannot stand against the disintegrating forces of globalization" and called for a similar disentanglement from the past.

"Radical contemporary changes in the church and society worldwide demand a completely new approach for the traditional ecumenical bodies... The Council must undergo a profound change and transform its way of thinking and acting and of organizing and renewing its work."

For the Orthodox prelate, globalization makes Christian relations with other faith communities a concern of "existential importance". Affirming Christianity's faith in Jesus Christ must not preclude engaging in dialogue and collaboration with other religions, Aram told the assembly.

As Tutu and Aram and other ecumenical leaders point to unity as the only hope for a transformed world, the divine *all*, how does the ecumenical movement and the WCC, its institutional expression, find the way to something radically new? Although WCC works closely with the Roman Catholic church, and has done for almost 40 years, through the Joint Working Group; though most Orthodox churches have been members for many years and it has intentional and growing contacts with Pentecostal and evangelical communities, they are not important financial supporters of the WCC or its ecumenical endeavours.

Confessional bodies, among them the LWF, WARC, the World Methodist Council, the Baptist World Alliance, the Salvation Army, the Anglican Consultative Council, Mennonites, Quakers, Pentecostal World Fellowship and the Ecumenical (Constantinople) and Moscow Patriarchates, make up Christian World Communions (CWCs) separately from the WCC. Many denominations that support confessional bodies also support the WCC and as their decline persists, choices will have to be made. If we are serious about broadening the ecumenical movement, compromises will almost certainly be required to include evangelicals and Pentecostals, while at the same time this greater inclusiveness would almost certainly cause problems for traditional churches, especially in the Orthodox family and the Vatican.

Should the WCC adjust or change its structures and governance to allow for the full participation of all these churches and many more in the ecumenical movement? Should we become the prime movement for a world-wide Christian jubilee without the sense of full "membership" which has been at the heart of WCC integrity for more than 50 years? It seems not only necessary, but urgent, to consider ways for manifesting the oneness, the inclusivity and coherence of Christianity beyond the WCC.

The same applies to other ecumenical organizations which cannot belong to the World Council: national councils of churches, regional ecumenical organizations and CWCs. They are "privileged partners" and can send (non-voting) delegates to assemblies but there are no recognized procedures to link and coordinate the process of policy-making and programme planning. This may be another place to raise again the idea of the Global Christian Forum (GCF) to serve the interest of greater coherence in the ecumenical movement.

But these various proposals lack the passion, the urgency and the optimism that Tutu and the abolitionists of slavery call us back to. There are dozens of reasons, constitutions, rules, protocols, commissions, committees, coalitions, movements, organizations, denominations, confessional bodies at all levels of Christianity, that can present undeniably learned, prudent and pragmatic reasons why this or that move towards a divine *all* just cannot be done. There really seems to be no passion for the unity that is the basis for the ninth assembly's call for world transformation.

The ecumenical movements and the whole of Christianity have too many institutions, organizations, structures, bureaucracies, all with vested interests, to create a new movement that is fully inclusive. To reconfigure the ecumenical movement requires much more than retooling structures and organizations to make them more efficient and vital, there must be a willingness, indeed an urgent demand for unity, that will allow Christianity to make the costly compromises with its historic church traditions and structures that are required as the story of the abolitionists of the slave trade tells us.

Yet many member churches are urgently asking us to work towards a consolidation of ecumenical structures beyond the local and national levels. Just think, for a moment, what the ecumenical jet set must face in almost any given year: delegates sent to world assemblies of several different organizations (the WCC met early in 2006, in the middle of the year another 5,000 delegates went to South Korea for the World Methodist Council, for many it will be their second major international church trip). There are countless meetings around issues such as the HIV and AIDS conferences in New York in May and Toronto in August where churches will be widely represented by both delegates and staff. Regional and national meetings go on plus a seemingly endless round of specialized meetings ranging from small working groups to full-fledged commissions to large international conferences of several hundreds or thousands.

Each of these events meeting in rapid succession receives and considers papers, information, recommendations and proposals, all of them deadly serious, but even full-time staff members of the WCC and the churches cannot keep track of the vast array of preparatory documents, books, worship materials, rules and regulations, press conferences, decisions and follow-up assignments that bear startling resemblance to the aforementioned Tower of Babel. What possible impact can this have on members of local congregations, despite the modern means of communications? Check any church website, then ask how many members have access to it and then how many have no idea what we are talking about or why we are holding all these meetings, many with the same delegates attending at enormous cost to discuss many of the same issues. And imagine the duplication of work, time and money. Could we not have a single ecumenical church assembly of a few hundred delegates to do the organizational work? And then perhaps a huge global celebration of people from the local churches to praise God with passion and optimism and inclusivity? A global forum of Christians saying a new world is possible?

That might be the first challenge facing WCC after Porto Alegre: no institutional reform or radical change will be successful unless it is guided and accompanied with a clear reaffirmation of the ecumenical vision for the third millennium disentangled from past structures and institutions.

Inter-religious dialogue

The American poet, Carl Sandburg (1878-1967) was once asked "what is the ugliest word in the English language?" After much thought, he answered: "exclusive".

The future of the ecumenical movement – which we have been warned is not eternal – will be determined by many things, of course, but it will be largely, and finally, determined by how much we wish to legitimize diversity and how sincere and energetic is our conviction that the dignity of our diversity and differences is indeed a divine mandate. History has created for us a society from which we cannot escape, rather it is our responsibility to build upon this inheritance and create a viable and vibrant movement of which we can all be proud. We need to recognize that the future of the movement is dependent entirely on our ability and commitment to live together for good and through mutual respect and understanding, encourage dialogue and cooperation among our many different communities. God is the author of our diversity.

It was a common enough topic at the ninth assembly across confessions and differences. People saw its urgency in many ways: Desmond Tutu's divine *all*; from Orthodox Archbishop Anastasios of Tirana and All Albania, church unity was "a duty and a necessity" in an age of globalization. "If there is not this direction towards diversity, it is a new scandal to the world." He stressed the WCC was a "forum for people" rather than an institution, a "forum of love and hope." Bishop Margot Kässman of the Evangelical Lutheran Church in Germany was "impatient" at today's ecumenism. "If we cannot recognize each other as churches what right have we to call all the peoples of the world to more unity, to celebrate our differences?"

Fearfully, many worried about phrases like the "clash of civilizations" being bandied about by western politicians in the corridors of power around the globe. The anti-Islam cartoons published just before the assembly started an anguished debate among liberals in the North and violent demonstrations in many parts of the world. Reviving old words like the mediaeval Christian Crusades to describe the wars of the West against terror and use of Jihad as a response has forced some to speak of world conflagration over religion and religious values.

Inter-religious dialogue was recognized as one of the most pressing needs for our time and perhaps the most pressing challenge for the ecumenical movement. In a globalized world, with rapidly shrinking and ever more porous borders between communities, religion has become an increasingly significant component in inter-communal relations. Faith, belief, can make things infinitely better or can make them alarmingly worse.

Dr Rowan Williams, the scholarly Archbishop of Canterbury and titular leader of the world-wide Anglican Communion, addressed this question in a plenary address to the ninth assembly, entitled "Christian Identity and Religious Plurality".

The question of Christian identity, Dr Williams said, seeks to ground it so firmly in the person of Jesus Christ that people of other religions, other faiths, would be seen neither as threats nor as targets. "The claim of Christian belief is not, first and foremost, that it offers the only accurate system of thought, as against all other competitors."

However, it is important to note that Williams was not saying that, "by standing in the place of Christ" in interfaith dialogue, Christians were taking a triumphalist stance or an attitude of conversion from the other's faith to Christianity.

"It is possible to live in such intimacy with God that no fear of failure can ever break God's commitment to us, and to live in such a degree of mutual gift and understanding that no human conflict or division need bring us to uncontrollable violence and mutual damage."

There are two unhelpful ways of approaching other faiths: either with an aggressive claim to exclusive possession of the truth, or with the loss of confidence leading to a view that every religion is as good as the other, Williams told the Assembly. The analysis may resonate with many Western countries, who have only relatively recently been faced with the reality of religious pluralism.

In other parts of the world, notably Asia, Christians, very often in the minority, have been wrestling with dialogue and its challenges and problems for many years. Wesley Ariarajah of Sri Lanka, with long experience in ecumenical interfaith dialogue, was part of an ecumenical "Conversation" at the ninth assembly:

"No religious tradition is isolated any longer," he said. There was a time when mission organizations from the North set out to convert the heathen and the pagan – anyone really who was not a Protestant Christian – confident to the point of arrogance that the faith in Christ that they preached should be embraced by all people. "Today," Ariarajah explains, "we are under growing pressure, if we are to survive violence and hatred, to live in mutual relationships. There is an irresistible plurality, a persistent plurality. Today we are called to form our identity in relation to other identities."

This means, it seems, a rethinking of word and action and dialogue, the very way in which we hold our beliefs. What is the relation between dialogue and doctrine? Can we Christians continue to say we have the only truth and then go to our Muslim or Jewish or Buddhist friends and say that we want to be in dialogue with you to find the truth. Inter-faith dialogue has a future only if we own the fundamentals of our faith in a new way, in the context of plurality.

Most of the fundamental ethical codes of the great religions are rooted in the insight that human life is community and, in relationship with Nature, can be sustained only on a basis of intentional self-limitation of power and greed. This acknowledgement of limits is based on an understanding of human existence as being in relationship. Each human person is a centre of relationships. Our identity is formed through our relationships with other human beings, within the natural environment and ultimately with God.

So, in a sense inter-religious dialogue becomes a "dialogue of life." Rowan Williams urged the assembly to remember the courage with which Christians are suffering while living as persecuted minorities in countries such as Egypt, Pakistan, India, the Balkans and Iraq and still trying to work with, and alongside, non-Christian neighbours. "This is not the climate of 'dialogue' as it happens in the West, or in the deeply comfortable and terribly polite settings of international conferences."

Inter-religious dialogue therefore can be a heady mix of academic and theological debate and discussion, or it can be a dangerous place where religious extremism, exclusion of minorities and competition for ideas and persons takes place. It is "both promising in dealing with a polarized world and a globalized world and also deeply risky. At the community level, people from different faiths often live together and dialogue together, they act together and respect differences, indeed celebrate them. Much like the Lund Principle (1952) for Christians working together who pledged "to do nothing separately that we could in conscience do together."

Many Christians today, however, fear that by acknowledging plurality they are watering down the faith and what they see as their evangelical obligation to convert. Williams doesn't see it that way: "When we face radically different notices, strange and complex accounts of a perspective not our own, our perspective must not be 'How do we convict them of error? How do we win the competition for ideas?' but 'What do they actually see? And can what they see be a part of the world that I see'?"

Differences and diversity, a terribly important theme for the ecumenical movement, has taken inter-religious dialogue out into the frightening and volatile world of today that the WCC has called God to help it transform. What can the WCC do as a global community to work in and recognize pluralism by working practically with Muslims, Jews, Hindus and Buddhists to face the long list of issues that came before the 2006 assembly: terrorism and counter terrorism, human rights, genocide, disease, reforming the UN, water for life, elimination of nuclear arms, trafficking in women and protection of children and the vulnerable, global warming and climate change, Indigenous People, people with disabilities, the devastation of the poor by globalization, loss of species, our commitment to Africa, Latin America and Asia – and the list goes on every day? We throw up our hands or we try to set a kind of moral triage – what devastation can we deal with and what do we ignore since the assembly told us to do better with less? Is that one solution, to do more than dialogue, to reach a point, and urgently, when we work together in faith, interfaith, to effect change or we may not survive?

There are already calls for inter-religious initiatives to support the work of the UN and its agencies. There are attempts to establish institutions similar to the UN, where representatives of world religions address conflicts. There are visions of religions setting up inter-religious emergency teams ready to intervene in faith when crises loom on the horizon.

There are multi-faith initiatives to articulate and formulate declarations on global ethics, human responsibilities and set guidelines for inter-religious interaction and commitments. The celebration of the UN Year of Dialogue among Civilizations (2001) was intended to provide an opportunity to emphasize that the present globalization process does not only encompass economic, financial and communications areas but it also brought a renewed focus on human, cultural and spiritual dimensions emphasizing the interdependence of humankind and its rich diversity.

Other inter-religious initiatives are expressed in conjunction with societal and global issues: injustice, poverty, violence and environmental destruction. Religions were being called upon, with immense hope, not to shirk their responsibilities for the planet, God's Creation. Alliances are being called for between faith and the economy, issue-oriented institutions and social movements on poverty, ecology and sustainable development. Through dialogue with political and economic leaders, religious leaders are invited to bring the moral authority of religions to help solve problems dividing communities and nations. Promoting peace, reconciliation and human progress are goals we all share.

The voice of religious peoples has been requested by both business and politics. The reasons may vary from a self-serving interest to get religions to justify this or that particular action, to a genuine interest in developing a dialogue with religion on issues of common concern. There are many in the UN leadership who express a wish that it may become a body which relates not only to its different member states but also to civil society, religions very much included.

A Conference on Interfaith Cooperation for Peace was organized at the UN headquarters in New York in 2005 under a tripartite partnership among governments, the UN system and civil society representing religious NGOs. It aimed at enhancing interfaith cooperation, promoting the culture of peace and dialogue among civilizations, as well as translating shared values into practical action. The conference drew inspiration from the UN Millennium Declaration and on-going efforts to promote interfaith cooperation at the international, interregional, regional and national levels. Part of the conference statement said:

"The UN has been called upon to recognize that dialogues between civilizations, cultures and religions constitute vital contributions towards the promotion of a just and sustainable peace. New ways must be identified to address inter-religious, intercultural and inter-civilizational issues and concerns, including the opportunity and mechanism for religious leaders to speak, interact and respond more clearly and quickly and with concerted voices in times of violence, crises and conflict."

Our world is one cloth, one seamless garment. To tear the thread of any one strand inevitably affects all of them together and shreds the whole cloth. Although it has become almost a meaningless slogan it is used so often, the fact is that there can be no peace without justice, no justice without peace. There have been dialogues between African Christians and Jews in recent years and in these talks they learned that *shalom* means not only "wholeness" but its roots can mean "to pay one's debts". In order to obtain the blissful condition of *shalom* wholeness, one must pay one's debts. And with respect to the longer commitment from our respective faiths, *shalom*, or *ubuntu* as Africans would put it, means almost the same thing in English.

Christian identity and religious plurality are interconnected subjects for a transformed World Council of Churches. It cannot be changed by jargon and clichés about tolerant coexistence of different opinions. It has to faced, as Rowan Williams put it to the Porto Alegre assembly, by recognizing that "the nature of our conviction as Christians puts us irrevocably in a certain place that is both promising and deeply risky, the place where we are called to show utter commitment to the God who is revealed in Jesus Christ and to all those to whom his invitation is addressed. Our very identity obliges us to active faithfulness of this two-fold kind. We are not called to win competitions or arguments in favour of our 'product' in some religious marketplace. Identify yourself! Identify our reasons for living, for living less badly and dying less badly. And we do so by giving prayerful thanks for our place and by living faithfully where God in Jesus has brought us to be, so that the world may see what is the depth and cost of God's own fidelity to the world God has made."

It seems time for the ecumenical movement to reconfigure itself, to face the painful truths we have learned about and to know that we do not face this future alone.

7. The beloved community*

A question that crops up in places like "ecumenical conversations" or the *mutirao* or in meetings and drafting public statements, almost anywhere where a group of church people get together, is the issue of why we Christians are so loth to talk about controversial issues, especially if we are bureaucrats or highly-placed leaders. It seems there are two basic reasons.

The first is that we really don't feel confident about what to say and how to say it straight and clear, so we couch it in soft words, covered like cotton wool and protected with the safety of ecuspeak or ecclesiastical jargon. Perhaps we are grossly under-informed which makes us nervous and that ignorance may be just because we are too complacent. But, for the ecumenical movement that is an ethical, not an intellectual, fault. We have many hundreds of people with whom we can consult all around the world. There are so many people who would be delighted to share their knowledge, wisdom and expertise with us, but it can't just be the same old people who tell us what we already know and why we can't say anything different. If we are from the North, we should make a point of listening regularly to people from the South. If we are from traditional denominations, we should have more discourse *with* not *about* Pentecostals and evangelicals. If we're men we should do the same with women. Straight people should talk more with gay and lesbian people rather than pretending they don't exist. And, of course, as we saw in chapter 6, we need close sympathetic "listening" discussions with Jewish, Muslim and other friends from different faiths. Then we can speak with clear-eyed, confident knowledge.

A second reason for avoiding controversial issues is the deep need of many Christian leaders to be liked, to be loved.

---

* In the language of the early Christians, *Basilea*, (the Greek word for "Kingdom") was the Church's ultimate dream and its most crucial hope. It evokes the vision of Jesus Christ for a radical community of hope and provides an alternative to the prevailing neo-liberal economic model. When Christians speak about the Beloved Community, the Kingdom of Heaven, they are describing the hope for a life in which our well-being is not determined by the whims of governments or corporations.

All of us benefit from true friends, those who are willing to risk their friendships for the sake of their friends. Quite different are those pastors and leaders who are fearful of saying anything that would imperil the love of their followers or members. That is not, of course, to say that we should not be pastoral in approaching a controversy. However, we need to remember that Jesus never withheld the telling of the truth just to avoid controversy. Saint Augustine once said that there are as many wolves *within* the fold as there are sheep *without*. Though the estimate may be surprising, the thought certainly is not. If the essence of evil is disguise – pretending something bad, like globalization, is really something good – and if the best disguise in the world is the cloak of religious piety, where else, if not in a church would you expect to find evil people? As the 17th century French philosopher, Blaise Pascal wrote: "People never do evil so cheerfully as when they do it from religious conviction." The point is, don't good shepherds of their flocks have a certain calling to drive out the wolves in order to make room for more sheep?

Ideally, we should stay engaged, both to our members and to the issues that vitally affect the lives of all of us.

If church leaders, individually and collectively, want their members to lend them their ears, they must first give them their hearts. And if they do, then because of their love for their members, they shall never be afraid to put at risk their love for them. Most people are far more prepared for painful truths than they are given credit for. What most want their leaders to do is to raise to a conscious level the knowledge inherent in their experience. And the majority of people realize that the painful truths known and spoken sour and subvert life less than those known and unspoken.

Perhaps the time for painful truths was February 2006 in Porto Alegre when His Holiness Aram I of Cilicia in his role as retiring Moderator for more than 14 years, bluntly told the 348 largely Protestant, Anglican and Orthodox churches from more than 100 countries that the WCC was in a state of "stagnation". And, perhaps that was why, in an era of global turmoil over religion, 4,000 people could meet and leave 10 days later without much acrimony. There were no walkouts or major divisions. Everything ran smoothly down in southern Brazil, from the air-conditioned hotels, to the air-conditioned buses, to the air-conditioned plenary hall and the five excellent dining rooms. Maybe "stagnant" was too strong a word for the US president of the United Church of Christ (UCC), John Thomas, who described the assembly as a transitional moment in Christian relations. But, a transition to what? From "stagnation" to what?

Hanging over the assembly was something called "relationships", a bureaucratic word that could mean anything but in the comfort of the Pontifical University's central campus there were many people conscious of the gaps in the global Christian community's largest institution of the ecumenical movement, despite it having some 560 million members worldwide. But, aside from those 4,000 at Porto Alegre, did many people in the pews know about the WCC or care much that it was meeting in the global South, in a country where Pentecostalism is growing like the wind, causing great anxiety for the once influential Roman Catholic Church?

Sheer numbers of active Pentecostals around the world, perhaps 400 million, especially in Africa and Latin America, are forcing the WCC to make overtures and to recognize the Pentecostal movement. Relationships, both formal and informal are paramount to WCC members but so far have not been built easily or quickly and can remain fragile. Some Pentecostals are interested, others are not. The WCC has not yet taken any concrete steps about membership that might result in Pentecostal churches and denominations joining the WCC but in Porto Alegre it did reflect on the nature of the ecumenical movement and stated that it needed to look beyond the "institution of ecumenism".

Some of the blunt truths also came from the knowledge that the WCC is losing members of course in the global North and also to new churches but even more blunt is that its income, also largely from the traditional Protestant churches in Europe and North America, has dropped by almost a third since the last assembly in Harare in 1998. "Do less and do it better" was a catch phrase from the Council's finance committee that resonated around the halls and will lead to programme cuts later when the new Central Committee meets. Focussing on a few core themes such as the fight against poverty, the continual environmental destruction of the planet and its species, peace and war and the global South will be the main programme work.

Some critics who love the WCC called it moribund and in danger of "ossifying". Is it? My answer is an emphatic no. Some say it is too leftish, espousing political causes that conservative Christians detest on such issues as war and poverty and globalization. However, it is unlikely the WCC will temper its much-needed prophetic voice. And it got a big boost from Brazil's President Luiz Inacio Lula Da Silva when he came to thank the WCC for its activism during his country's long 20-year struggle to democracy. "During those long, hard years we found in the World Council of Churches not only moral and spiritual support, but also active solidarity."

This too, is speaking truth without compromise. As the Council moves towards its 60th birthday, it finds its 1948 principal aim of formally unifying the global Christian community being forced by a new world ideology called globalization into something it calls reconfiguration. This would carry forward a vision or visions of the ecumenical movement in the 21st century and the structures it will need. Reconfiguration is "church-driven" not Geneva or headquarters-driven. It is intended to broaden the movement, deepen the fellowship and deal with the vexed question of strengthening relationships. Some critics say reconfiguration is simply another of the Council's attempts to restructure itself, a process that already has produced the Common Understanding and Vision (CUV) and reduced staff, cut expenses and tried to make more flexible the heavy European style of management inherited from the past. Certainly that element will have to be there but reconfiguration is really about "the future of ecumenism in the 21st century". And it is urgent because the beginning of the third millennium has consolidated a new ideology for which many post-world second world war international organizations such as the UN and WCC were ill-prepared.

Attack against multilateralism

Change is always hard for big and old structures dominated by representation and, while the world has moved to an ideology of control and domination, the ecumenical movement and its Council is still driven by a world of ideas, polite discourse and theological discussions about how to "facilitate" constructive change in society. And, it has had some major successes over the decades.

However this new ideology is not about facilitating constructive change, it is about radical neo-conservatism, about a world where people and resources are manipulated and used through brute forces such as violence, war, confrontation, competition, efficiency etc. The use of force by coalitions of armed partners with the lone superpower who interprets the world by setting up "new enemies of humanity" to legitimize the culture of violence is the *modus operandi*. At a time when secularism is at its peak in the global North, the process of naming the enemies is filled with religious and spiritual symbolism, using "good" and "evil" to indicate that God is on one side and Satan on the other.

Fear, insecurity, anxiety, characterize the lives of many millions of people, even those in the materially affluent world. People feel threatened, confused and extremely unsettled. Technology, the 21st century's answer to old fears of disease, poverty and insecurity has instead been turned to new and ever-more sophisticated weapons of control – armaments that are "smarter" than people; economics operated by electronic systems of domination devoid of human aspirations; and cultures homogenized by networks of communication to promote a materialism that is soul-destroying. The quest for domination and control is to guarantee the security of the globalized economy, controlled by the nations of the G8 group of most developed countries – the richest nation states in the world. But these weapons of mass destruction proliferating across the world to the poor and not-so-rich nations make evident the prophetic warning of former US President Dwight Eisenhower in 1961 against the control of the world by the "military-industrial complex" of his country.

This new ideology increases the hegemony of all aspects of our world under the economic, political and military agendas instead of meeting the basic human needs of all – food, water, shelter, education and health. We are witnessing the emergence of the military state that Eisenhower predicted, justified by the spin doctors of globalized communications whose primary aim is regime change.

Institutions like the WCC and UN, whose very existence is based on the concept and growth of multilateralism, now find the ideal under attack, weakened and undermined as an instrument of global peace and security. Consumed by those hegemonic desires, the advocates of globalization are constantly engaged in redesigning a world in which the poor and the weak have little or no voice. Indeed, they are often blamed for their own plight. In the name of national security for wealthy nations, people are being persecuted for wishing to improve their lives through migration. Screening, detention, national identification cards that violate people's privacy are increasingly fashionable in the industrialized world. The vulnerability of nation states, especially in the South, extends to the weakening of the civic public realm and capacity for alternative frameworks of engagement.

These new forms of tyranny are more difficult for multilateral institutions because they derive their legitimacy and authority from popular, if badly skewed, western style democracy. A big part of the prophetic task of the ecumenical movement in the 21st century must be to assist human communities in finding ways of going beyond the logic of violence and domination and establishing alternative ways of resolving conflicts.

A new epoch for ecumenism?

Another area where multilateral organizations have been unprepared is that of ethical human understanding and acting. The reconfiguration process will identify a new path for the ecumenical movement to identify and address the issues and dilemmas facing today's world. The process is intended not only to promote greater respect for human rights but also the enhancement of a new culture of peace and justice for preventing and overcoming all forms of violence. This means a redefined ecumenical engagement with the challenges and opportunities facing the church in this third millennium.

During the last decades, the Council has also had to face, often reluctantly, a new way of promoting human development with the arrival on the world scene of non-governmental organizations (NGOs) which quickly replaced churches and a few philanthropies in responding to human need. Their storming onto the world scene in an informal and at first often unorganized way has been so phenomenal that even governments, let alone the churches, are in competition for resources with the NGOs. While it seems that some NGOs are exhausting the social space and are being challenged by the complexities and politics of resource mobilization, the institutional church is also facing new challenges posed by the emergence of non-denominational forms of ecumenical congregations.

Almost all of the formal arrangements, institutional structures and prerogatives of ecumenism have been challenged, forcing – if it is to survive – what some are calling a new epoch. The new forms of challenge, which are primarily experiential forms of faith, come from all over the world and are in clear defiance of what is seen as the over-bureaucratization of historic denominations. Not since the days of the Reformation have we seen such suspicion of church institutions and structures. People are leaving these institutions for more informal expressions of faith such as Pentecostalism, mega- and storefront churches, and post-denominational churches. They are attractive to youth and also to the developing world who more and more reject the hierarchical ties originating with colonialism and the mission churches. Liberal denominations advance theological and doctrinal positions that clash with the cultural norms. There is a void in modern ways of expressing faith that invites more creative, less bureaucratic and more relation-ship-oriented values in Christian living.

Underlying this challenge is a search for an "authentic" spirituality which connects people with their humanity. The issue is how post-modernity continues to alienate human beings from their own humanity. Without our basic human drive to relate and share with one another, Christianity would not make much sense. If post-modernity is threaten-ing to rob us of our capacity to be human, then how can we claim to be Christians? The ecumenism of the last century came out of student movements, and the streams of Faith and Order, and Life and Work of the past, but can no longer be relevant or sustained by those movements which, them-selves, are in need of transformation to meet the needs of the 21st century.

Assuming this search for spirituality among youth, both North and South, is an authentic global phenomenon, can we take for granted that many young Christians want to adhere to their faith and are seeking for profound meaning in life? There is no clear answer to this question: some young people naturally reject religious traditions as irrele-vant, out-of-date and with little to support them in leading moral and meaningful lives in an age when almost every-thing traditional is under threat; others seek the kind of spirituality that is activist with movements for peace, against poverty, trying to build a better world by opposing global-ization. Huge, sometimes violent, rallies of youth from all over the world have been held in opposition to the interna-tional financial meetings and the International Monetary Fund and World Bank, organized with great skill and pas-sion by hundreds of thousands of people allied with the World Social Forum. Organized and institutionalized Chris-tianity is not there, nor is it in traditional Protestant and Roman Catholic churches, except in rare instances.

Those who know about the fourth assembly of the WCC held in Uppsala, Sweden (1968), will know that church youth virtually took over the assembly, demanding from their elders a role in decision-making, pushing the ecumenical movement to take young people seriously, demanding an agenda of social justice. They were noisy, irreverent to their church elders, frustrated by the rule of order and backroom control exercised by professional ecumenists. It was rough, unlike the smooth and managed operation of the ninth, but the WCC came out of Uppsala with perhaps the most relevant and radical agenda it has ever had: the Programme to Combat Racism, the church's own airlift into eastern Nigeria to feed millions of starving Biafrans and a direction that clearly put the ecumenical movement on a course of transforming the world at that time. It would be repeated again in 1975 at Nairobi, but there was growing anxiety about the WCC's straying too far from theology and doctrine and into the messy politics of the world. Gradually the youth grew up and went elsewhere and WCC structures hunkered down in processes and procedures. This is not to say that spirituality in the WCC was ever in doubt. The Orthodox families of churches have always stressed this.

Now, there is a sense that some youth at least want to come back, want to find a space for dialogue and action about the great issues of the third millennium. Many talk of a spiritual yearning and the ecumenical movement must relate organically for that more experiential dimension of faith. Two examples occurred in 2004.

- A group of young Danish people visiting the Ecumenical Centre in Geneva one day, described to me their search for a more profound meaning to life than that found in their affluent, hi-tech, materialistic society. But they were conducting this search for spirituality outside the traditional values of their churches. For them, the old forms of religion were hollow, did not speak to their needs in their own context. There was not enough substance. What is it that so many established churches and religions are failing to provide? Organized religion does not always equate with spirituality.

- The Nairobi Chapel in the capital of Kenya is arguably the fastest-growing congregation in my country. Growing from a small university chapel which a decade ago had only a handful of worshippers, Nairobi Chapel today holds four services a weekend and a midweek service that are all packed with young Kenyans, most of whom have left the traditional churches of their parents and rejected denominationalism. There are Anglicans, Roman Catholics, Methodists, Presbyterians who now simply call themselves Christians who come together to celebrate their commonality. Most are well-educated professionals who have embarked on a dynamic process of living their beliefs with energy and action.

Post-denominationalism

Places like the Nairobi Chapel, and there are many, are part of a phenomenon called post-denominationalism and many traditional churches fear it. Traditional denominations may be on the endangered species list, but others aren't forecasting extinction, unless there is an inability or refusal to change. More accurately descriptive words might be "transitional" or even "neo"-denominationalism. The question facing institutional, highly structured religion is what churches are going to look like in the 21st century.

Many denominations are under radical reconstruction right now and often aren't even aware of it:

- the increasing use of generic church names which leave out denominational affiliation;

- the explosive growth of para-church groups, which are attracting time, energy and resources away from local churches. Many of these groups are big on worship and service, but have minimal theological or doctrinal stances so they can appeal to a wide variety of people from different denominations;

- a shift from a focus on long-term global mission investments to short-term mission projects often initiated at the local church level, sometimes partnered with denominations who provide short-term mission opportunities without losing a global focus;

- the rapid increase in use of the internet and desktop publishing, which has created an "entrepreneurial spirit" in some churches when it comes to producing Christian resources. It has eroded support for, or use of, religious publishing houses; and

- denominational conflicts that have resulted in numerous "smaller niche" schools, forcing many seminaries to close, merge or seriously evaluate their curriculum and training methods needed for the 21st century.

In addition to waning denominational loyalty, "post-modernism" and "generational challenges" contribute to post-denominationalism

Post-modernism puts the ecumenical movement and its traditional member churches in a time frame of change intellectually. Since the Enlightenment in the 1700s, reason and rationality ruled for 300 years. Most theologians and thinkers were influenced by it, but in the new era, there's been a major transition in the way people think.

While the Enlightenment affirmed the idea that the human capacity for knowledge was unlimited, the post-modern mind sees limits and, as a result, post-modern thinking has trouble with concepts like absolute truth and universal identities. Authoritarian structures are mistrusted, holding contradictory ideas is acceptable and tolerance is lifted up as a virtue.

The post-modern mind is very accepting of pluralism and the buzzword among many young people is "spirituality" not "religion". For many spiritual searchers, such as the young Danish group which came to visit me at the WCC, any religion is acceptable as long as it speaks to one's spirit.

As a result, much of Europe and North America – and in a different way the global South such as the Nairobi Chapel – has developed a "consumer religion" where people "shop" for the church that meets their practical and experiential, not theological, needs.

Most institutional and traditional churches have fostered this consumerism by not providing people with balanced discipleship. Some things have been left out and people are trying to fill those holes with something else, often something secular with a gloss of religion. For example, corporations and even armies now commonly have widely publicized "mission" statements, taking the cue from churches about "spiritual" goals and objectives, although often a disguise for their true motivation.

Another result of the post-denominational and post-modern world is a loss of denominational distinctions, particularly for young people. Just a few years ago, in an ecumenical movement which was trying to bring about unity, it was common to identify individuals by denomination and it was clear what the differences were between Lutherans and Methodists, Anglican and Orthodox, Reformed and Roman Catholic but today, even in the Orthodox and Roman Catholic churches, perhaps the most traditional, denominational lines have been blurred.

Many of today's young people have no knowledge of basic denominational beliefs and doctrines. Identity for many young people is more among their friends, families, peer groups, schools, sports, and much less their denomination, even if they acknowledge having one.

Some denominations will remain and they will remain relevant. For a denomination to be the most relevant, it needs to be able to empower local churches and people. And the churches and denominations who are able to maintain allegiance to the unchanging gospel, but who find unique ways to transmit it, are the ones who are going to survive and meet the needs of restless, searching young people.

With all this flux, the process of ecumenism in the third millennium must take seriously these realities which are already upon us and, indeed, have been with us for some time. They obviously call for a new ecumenical engagement that goes far beyond traditional bilateral dialogues to embrace wholeheartedly local spiritual needs. The time has come for the ecumenical movement and its leadership to consider seriously and as a matter of urgency what are the challenges which these local realities pose to the ecumenical conciliar bodies such as national councils of churches and regional ecumenical organizations. These, in turn, must accept challenges and develop capacities to assist the churches in articulating the relationship of self-understanding (ecclesiastical) and self-representation (ecclesiology) among different churches and communities.

Global Alliance for Development

Marking a new stage in ecumenical efforts to overcome poverty and injustice, churches and related organizations have agreed to move ahead with the establishment of a new global alliance for development. The changing world context and impact of globalization require that churches combine their efforts for witness and service and for peace and justice. Diakonia (service) is central to the mission and being of the churches and guided by the prophetic tradition, the ecumenical movement is compelled to see justice as the essence of the love of God in our critique of the destructive impact of injustice and misuse of power.

The new alliance offers the ecumenical movement an opportunity to create something new, something which lives out the principles Christians all uphold, something which strengthens the movement.

"A collective analysis and response by the ecumenical family to the problems we face in Africa and elsewhere is absolutely necessary," confirmed Bishop Mvume Dandala, general secretary of the Nairobi-based All Africa Conference of Churches. But he warned that any new initiative must be primarily focused on local empowerment and the building of "self-confidence" of people and churches.

"There is a definite need and common interest for ecumenical partners to move from isolated initiatives to a coordinated approach, especially in the face of critical problems like HIV/AIDS," agreed Rev. Cornelia Füllkrug-Weitzel, director of Bread for the World, one of Germany's main church aid agencies.

Studies confirm that the WCC and its related agencies form potentially one of the largest international networks for development. At a consultation in 2005 those present anticipated that increased coordination and more strategic collaboration between participants in the alliance could increase their effectiveness in addressing issues of poverty and injustice. It is also hoped that the alliance will enhance the visibility of ecumenical organizations in the area of development.

The alliance will have a close relationship with ACT International, the WCC-related coordination body for emergency relief, and with the Ecumenical Advocacy Alliance (EAA), a broad ecumenical network of 90 ecumenical agencies for international cooperation in advocacy on global trade and HIV and AIDS.

ACT (Action by Churches Together) Development, as it has been named, will be a global alliance of church-related development agencies so that the ecumenical movement can do more effective work in a coordinated fashion that will reduce duplication and confusion.

Negotiations and consultations with more than 50 church agencies have been long and arduous. WCC will play a leading role in the new alliance including:

- interpreting the alliance to its broad constituency;
- convening the executive committee for an interim period at the outset;
- housing ACT Development in the WCC for up to five years; and
- providing the global platform for the discussion of major issues within the context of commissions or advisory groups.

Beyond these formal arrangements, WCC will have a close programmatic relationship which will complement the work of the Council in an integrated way. This will combine advocacy with theological reflection to enhance unity and mission which strengthens the relationship between ecumenical diakonia, advocacy and work for justice and uses innovative methodologies to bring together work at the grassroots and global levels. The world is changing and the WCC's ways of working must change with it.

Diakonia, advocacy and work for justice have the greatest potential for overlap between the alliance and WCC. There is far more work to be done in these areas than WCC could support but it does expect to play a lead role because these are the core areas of its mandate. Specialized Ministries and the WCC should set priorities and plan together to build on their strengths and avoid duplication. The ecumenical movement and its witness to those suffering the effects of injustice will be weakened if WCC and ACT Development take contradictory or opposing positions on specific issues.

The relationship of diakonia (service) to the life of the churches is not something that can be implemented by professionals coming in from outside. Diakonia is central to the mission and being of the churches, so the work of the alliance must not weaken the diaconal work of churches or cause divisions between churches. Instead, ACT Development must strengthen ecumenical diakonia, support ongoing relationships and create new ones. Closer relationships will need to be forged between WCC, ACT International and the Ecumenical Advocacy Alliance than have existed in the past where tensions over jurisdiction and working styles have been evident.

This is also the case for work in justice and advocacy so that the efforts are complementary and reinforcing. Justice without advocacy cannot exist and advocacy is essential for the transformational development to which the ecumenical movement aspires. Prophetic diakonia includes work for justice and advocacy.

WCC is a natural place for theological reflection and more is needed, particularly in the area of political ethics. However, theological reflection without action is in serious danger of becoming merely a think tank out of touch with local realities. Any notion that WCC should be relegated to theological reflection alone while ACT Development does the work on the ground must be rejected.

It is in the area of relationships with churches, ecumenical organizations of all kinds, Christian World Communions and other faith-based and secular organizations, with the UN and lay spiritual communities, that WCC is uniquely placed. Building relationships is central to development.

If this new initiative is to be a truly North-South instrument then the voice of the South (and the East) must be heard and taken seriously. The impetus for ACT Development came from the North – from agencies and specialized ministries – and the South is justifiably asking what is really behind it all. There is suspicion about the agencies' true motivation because, while the South can see the advantages the alliance can bring in strengthening their work, they are also aware that expectations are different between North and South and from the origins of ACT Development. Expectations may be different but they must also be accommodated if we are to create something new, something which lives out the principles we all uphold, something which strengthens us all. In the WCC, it is well known that struggling with different interests is not easy, but we can affirm that it is well worth the effort. The voices of the Southern partners must be heard when they question why some Specialized Ministries are operational, rather than working through the local partners.

One of the great buzzwords these days in ecumenical circles is "mutual accountability" but the willingness and commitment to change requires serious work if ACT Development is to be more than a good idea.

The alliance must also struggle with complex issues to develop membership criteria and it must be a frank and open discussion. From the experience of dealing with this issue in ACT International it is clear the very concept and meaning of membership is not clear. Some wish for a limited membership, others are looking for a more inclusive alliance.

This initiative has had a long and difficult history. For eight years it struggled before coming to some understanding. The ninth assembly has approved it in principle as a proposal. It is an important part of the reconfiguration discussions. We are committed to bringing the new baby into life, but if it is to be successful, it will require commitment and creativity and that won't happen if we try to serve our own institutional interests.

It will only happen when we seek to become more effective instruments in serving the causes of justice and peace in the world.

The spirituality of engagement

Spirituality too often is misunderstood as something that exists over and against religion, especially traditional organized Christianity as a religion. This is the greatest challenge facing ecumenism in the 21st century and its use in contemporary religious discourse requires deep analysis if it is not to provide one more enticement to battle-weary church leaders and members to retreat from social action and public controversy. If people are obsessed with the purely "spiritual", it could well mean that our theology and practice will once again turn inwards.

Perhaps a better definition for this issue of spirituality is one of identity which is something that almost always arises when we talk about issues of interchurch cooperation and interfaith dialogue. It is also something that affects people in their personal and public lives. Unlike the 20th century, which was dominated by the politics of ideology, the 21st century seems already to be dominated by the politics of identity. Who are we? What is the meaning of our lives, our relationships to God and to one another? How can we explore the "depth dimension" of human existence? Over the last two decades, it has become "politically correct" in public and media circles to speak of "spirituality" in positive terms, while use of the term "religion" often breeds suspicion and contempt.

The problem with the contemporary concept of "spirituality" is that too often it embraces a vaguely psychological orientation towards the search for identity and meaning. It often presents itself as an adjunct to the therapeutic, but in an uncritical self-affirming way. Indeed, in Western culture, the "self" can easily become the object of an ill-defined egoistic spirituality. American mythologist Joseph Campbell's mantra to "follow your bliss", has been used as a justification for selfishness and self-centredness – when it could as easily be interpreted as an invitation to discover the bliss of engaging creatively with the world.

John Wesley, the founder of Methodism, once observed that "the Bible knows nothing of solitary religion." To the extent that "spirituality" threatens to turn a new generation further inward, to focus minds on self, to exalt the solitary, then ecumenical Christianity has an important word to say. And an important part of our ecumenical calling today is to face the challenge of an ingrown spirituality and promote its alternative – a spirituality that rejoices in the continuity of things of the spirit with action for liberation, justice and peace. The discovery of identity, meaning and purpose must not be accepted as our ultimate goal. It is simply a spiritual starting point...

In 1975, M.M. Thomas of India, then moderator of the World Council of Churches' central committee, spoke of the need for a "spirituality of combat" in confronting the principalities and powers of this life. What is badly needed today is a spirituality of engagement that takes hold of real-world as well as personal challenges, and will not let them go unresolved.

Such a spirituality of engagement may begin in a profound encounter with the self, yet from the beginning, we must be prepared to move beyond self into close community and from there into action in the world God loves. In the solitude of self, we experience a yearning for companionship; in community, we find the desire and commitment to help build a much more just and caring world. In our interaction with the world and its people, the Holy Spirit will affirm our identity as followers of Jesus Christ.

The primary question that faces the ecumenical movement today is how we respond to the very serious challenges ahead. It helps to remember that what appear to be stumbling blocks may turn out to be stepping stones. It helps even more to realize that we do not face these challenges alone. The Triune God is with us, gathering and guiding us in company with the whole people of God.

The prayer, which was the theme for the ninth assembly of the WCC: "God, in your grace, transform the world" is at the centre of the ecumenical movement. Although many people spend a great deal of time contemplating the reconfiguration of existing institutions, or the founding of a more inclusive forum, the ecumenical movement is not ultimately about any of these structures. It is fundamentally about faith in God – proclamation of new life in Christ, confidence in the Spirit to lead us into visible expressions of the unity we possess as God's gift to the church.

The ecumenical movement is also a declaration, despite many of the challenges that face us, of our sure and certain hope for God's gracious transformation of the world.

An invitation to prayer

God, in your grace, transform the world

God of grace,
together we turn to you in prayer, for it is you who unite
    us:
you are the one God – Father, Son and Holy Spirit – in
    whom we believe,
you alone empower us for good,
you send us out across the earth in mission and service in
    the name of Christ.

We confess before you and all people:
We have been unworthy servants.
We have misused and abused the creation.
We have wounded one another by divisions everywhere.
We have often failed to take decisive action against
    environmental destruction, poverty, racism, caste-ism,
    war and genocide.
We are not only victims but also perpetrators of violence.
In all this, we have fallen short as disciples of Jesus Christ
who in his incarnation came to save us and teach us how
    to love.
Forgive us, God, and teach us to forgive one another.

God, in your grace, transform the world.

God, hear the cries of all creation,
the cries of the waters, the air, the land and all living
    things;
the cries of all who are exploited, marginalized, abused and
    victimized,
all who are dispossessed and silenced, their humanity
    ignored,
all who suffer from any form of disease, from war
and from the crimes of the arrogant who hide from the
    truth,
distort memory and deny the possibility of reconciliation.
God, guide all in seats of authority towards decisions of
    moral integrity.

God, in your grace, transform the world.

We give thanks for your blessings and signs of hope that
    are already present in the world,
in people of all ages and in those who have gone before us
    in faith;
in movements to overcome violence in all its forms, not
    just for a decade but for always;
in the deep and open dialogues that have begun both
    within our own churches and with those of other faiths
    in the search for mutual understanding and respect;
in all those working together for justice and peace –
both in exceptional circumstances and every day.
We thank you for the good news of Jesus Christ, and the
    assurance of resurrection.

God, in your grace, transform the world.

By the power and guidance of your Holy Spirit, O God,
may our prayers never be empty words
but an urgent response to your living Word –
in non-violent direct action for positive change,
in bold, clear, specific acts of solidarity, liberation, healing
    and compassion,
readily sharing the good news of Jesus Christ.
Open our hearts to love and to see that all people are made
    in your image,
to care for creation and affirm life in all its wondrous
    diversity.

Transform us in the offering of ourselves so that we may
    be your partners in transformation
to strive for the full, visible unity of the one Church of
    Jesus Christ,
to become neighbours to all,
as we await with eager longing the full revelation of your rule
in the coming of a new heaven and a new earth.

God, in your grace, transform the world. In the name of
    the Father, Son and Holy Spirit.
Amen.

(The official message to the world from the Ninth Assembly of the
World Council of Churches, meeting in February 2006 at Porto Alegre,
Brazil in the first decade of the third millennium, in the first assembly of
the WCC held in Latin America, took the form of a prayer.)

Acknowledgements

Many people were involved in the analysis and subsequent challenges that this book tries to set out. It is not an academic or even narrowly theological work, rather it is a distillation of many hours of dialogue with people around the world, more specifically in all the regions of the ecumenical movement. These include Africa, Asia, the Caribbean, Europe, Latin America, the Middle East, North America and the Pacific. For many of these meetings I deliberately set up questions and challenges that would provoke sometimes heated discussion and straightforward responses. On other occasions, when I had been specifically asked to speak about the future of ecumenism, I raised issues about dialogue, inclusion, exclusion, diversity, change, governance, institutions and how the structures and choices affect the lives of people longing for hope and healing, yearning for peace and harmony in a world where change comes faster than answers.

So I must thank hundreds upon hundreds of people from all over the planet who shared their insights and challenges. It was not always what we might have wanted to hear, for the ecumenical movement is seen by some as irrelevant or moribund or stagnant. So, many people, recognizing that hope lies in unity, spoke bluntly about our need for change and I have felt grateful for their honesty, obligated to reflect in the book what they said and what I spoke about. It is not easy reading if we are simply looking for something comfortable.

I am especially grateful for the support given me by the moderator of the central committee for the past two terms of some 15 years. His Holiness, Aram I, Catholicos of the Armenian Apostolic Church (Cilicia) was moderator until the end of the ninth assembly. His experience, wisdom and forthright understanding of the WCC and the ecumenical movement can be felt throughout the book.

Special thanks go to my wife, Ruth, for her support and inspiration. Very often I discussed new ideas with her and her comments, suggestions and critique helped me to see them in a new perspective. She accompanied me on several of my visits and she was always ready with suggestions which improved my speeches and writings.

Hugh McCullum, a Canadian writer and editor, has had years of experience with ecumenism in Africa and many other parts of the world, including a long association with WCC communications. I am most thankful for his work in organizing and editing *Called to the One Hope* and for providing me with the modern day parables, which make up the middle chapter of the book.

My thanks also to my colleague Ursula Zierl who made possible much of the logistics and recently retired Libby Visinand of WCC communications for technical assistance. Several of my programme colleagues contributed from their professional know-how by providing talking points for my speeches, and I wish to thank them very sincerely.

Glossary

AACC	All Africa Conference of Churches
ACN	Anglican Communion Network
ACT	Action by Churches Together
AIDS	acquired immune deficiency syndrome
AU	African Union
CUV	Common Understanding and Vision
CWCs	Christian World Communions
DOV	Decade to Overcome Violence
ECUSA	Episcopal Church in the USA
EAA	Ecumenical Advocacy Alliance
GCF	Global Christian Forum
HIV	human immunodeficiency virus
LRA	Lord's Resistance Army
LWF	Lutheran World Federation
MDGs	Millennium Development Goals (UN)
NGOs	Non-Governmental Organizations
PCR	Programme to Combat Racism
UN	United Nations
WARC	World Alliance of Reformed Churches
WCC	World Council of Churches
WSF	World Social Forum